Praise for *Teachers These Days*

"Education is arguably the most taxing profession on the planet. As teachers, we are simply tired. Recharging, refocusing, and reconnecting with our 'why' is the only way we'll survive the demands of the job. Dr. Jody Carrington and Laurie McIntosh do just that. Each page of *Teachers These Days* can only be described as cathartic."

—Joe Dombrowski, kindergarten teacher
and stand-up comedian

"I couldn't put it down. I loved the stories of other educators' experiences and the way each chapter ended with a question, a quote, and things to try. It is nice to be given actual strategies and advice on how to move forward. I really appreciated the emphasis on recognizing your privilege and how we cannot ignore race and racism any longer."

—Helen Vangool, teacher

"*Teachers These Days* is filled with heartfelt happies and heart-breaking hurts. I connect with the theory-into-practice way that it is set up, and I appreciated the voices of the others in their raw, poignant stories."

—Barbara Gruener, teacher and school counselor

"*Teachers These Days* honors the work and experience of educators while providing a familiar context to all teachers. The section on grief is captivating and visceral and beautiful. Thank you both so much for sharing this work, your words, and your wisdom."

—Meaghan Reist and Shelley Smith, vice principals
and creators of Culture Curators EDU

D0188378

"I've fallen in love with these ladies over and over again throughout the last few years. They keep challenging me to find my purpose, renew my passion, and focus on connection, all while reminding me I'm not alone. Listening to the stories of other educators has created a spark in me to continue connecting with other teachers so we can all continue to 'walk each other home.'"

—Carly Goruk, teacher

"*Teachers These Days* is a powerful testament to the impact teachers have on children each and every day. It is a book that speaks from experience but, most importantly, it comes from the heart. It will have you laughing one moment and tearing up the next. It has the potential to dramatically change your life perspective."

—Chris Smeaton, retired superintendent, leadership coach, and consultant

"Reading *Teachers These Days*, the word that comes to mind is passion. You can feel it radiate from every one of the stories here—stories written by educators just like me. It's a reminder that sometimes all you need to do is take a step back, take a breath, and look around—for those opportunities for connection with the students we work with but also with the adults in our buildings. The book is a gift filled with Dr. Jody and Laurie's knowledge and insight, and I already know I will be revisiting the calls to action at the end of each chapter time and time again throughout the year."

—Stephanie Power, educational assistant

Teachers These Days

Teachers
These Days

STORIES & STRATEGIES
FOR RECONNECTION

JODY CARRINGTON, PhD
LAURIE MCINTOSH, BEd

Teachers These Days: Stories & Strategies for Reconnection
© 2021 Jody Carrington, PhD, and Laurie McIntosh, BEd

This book is available at special discounts when purchased in quantity for educational purposes or for use as premiums, promotions, or fundraisers. For inquiries and details, contact the publisher at books@impressbooks.org.

Published by IMPress, a division of Dave Burgess Consulting, Inc.
IMPressbooks.org
DaveBurgessConsulting.com
San Diego, CA

Library of Congress Control Number: 2021941641
Paperback ISBN: 978-1-948334-36-5
Ebook ISBN: 978-1-948334-37-2

Cover design by Dr. Milena Radzikowska and Chris Shaddock
Interior design by Liz Schreiter
Editing and production by Reading List Editorial: readinglisteditorial.com

teacher noun

teach·er | \ ˈtē-chər
> 1. one who instructs by precept, example, or experience
> 2. one who guides the study of
> 3. one who imparts knowledge

If this definition describes you, we're so glad you're here. We know that in the education system, the "teacher" is the primary instructor and that teaching is a craft that takes years to build. We deeply honor this. We deliberately chose the title *Teachers These Days* because we believe that we are all teachers. Some of our best teachers have not been educators or instructors in a classroom, lab, or lecture hall; they have been bus drivers, custodians, hockey coaches, our best friend's mom. And some have, of course, been our school teachers, tenured or not. What we believe to the core is that we are all teachers and that very few of you know just how holy you are.

Contents

Introduction

A Note from Jody

My first attempt at writing a book resulted in a self-published best seller. I released *Kids These Days* on a wing and a prayer on February 14, 2019, after printing ten thousand copies and storing them in my garage. It was a book from the heart, by a psychologist (me), that held the stories of some of the toughest kids I've seen or worked with across Canada. It was written for educators, parents, leaders, clinicians—anyone, really, who knows or loves a kid. It's full of the stories that shaped me as a psychologist, a mom, a wife, and a woman, who is convinced that my purpose on this planet is to bravely reconnect the world (a small goal, really) by showing (not telling) my own babies how to do it. I wrote a lot of it with educators in mind because some of my greatest mentors have been teachers.

After twelve years of postsecondary education, it was clear to me that many of my professors and advisors had more impact on my views than my parents did. And as my own three children entered the world of education, I became acutely aware of the significant ways educators get woven into the tapestry of the lives of babies just like mine. I knew this to be true for me, too. Having grown up attending a K–12 school in rural Viking, Alberta, I can still tell you the first and last name of every teacher I had. I knew where they lived. I knew which ones liked me and which ones didn't. I babysat for at least three of them. When I see any one of them today, I am transported back to that little town that shaped so much of who I am. Teachers are sacred souls, and so many of them—so many of you—don't know just how powerful they are.

The whole premise of *Kids These Days* was based on what I knew as a child psychologist: Kids these days face a litany of unique issues and challenges. But kids are not the problem. As is true of every generation, the kids are only going to be OK if those of us holding them are OK. If we are connected, confident, and feel supported when (not if) we struggle at this whole raising-the-next-generation thing, then, and only then, will the kids, these aspiring adults, stand a chance. Here's the thing: we big people need to be connected, too. And therein lies the problem: today, we are more disconnected than ever.

When I started to speak across North America about *Kids These Days*, I was amazed—shocked, really— to find that my words resonated with so many people. Foremost among these was the line, "The next time you call a kid 'attention-seeking,' change it to 'connection-seeking' and see how your perspective changes." I get notes and emails from people around the world who say that this single sentence helped them reframe their work with kids in their classrooms and their homes. I started to wonder: Do those teachers know how much they matter?

Turns out, teachers of all students want more. In particular, they want more specific strategies on how to stay connected and get reconnected in any and all places where knowledge is imparted. When I was writing *Kids These Days*, an advisory board of amazing educators talked with me about how mental health issues show up in their schools. That was my jam, and I could discuss the mental health pieces all day. When educators started asking about what to do *in* the classroom, however, I knew I didn't have the answers.

Enter an educator hero of mine, one George Couros. A fellow Canadian, George has written books and created quite a following with his message of innovation in the classroom. One day, he came to watch me speak, and I spent a lot of that talk wondering what he was thinking. Afterward, he told me it was good and asked if I wanted feedback. To be honest, I didn't, but he gave it to me anyway. And I'm so glad he did, because his advice led me here, to my second book. He said the teachers he's worked hard to support, understand, and inspire are also very interested in *how* to do things. As a classroom teacher for fifteen years himself, George relied heavily on others to provide specific strategies and resources that worked not just in theory, but *in* the classroom. He pointed out the difference between me, a clinician who can talk all about emotions, and an educator, who is on the ground every day. Educators would benefit so much from specific suggestions they could tailor to their classrooms and student populations and that would fit their personalities and visions for their students. Every year classrooms change—staff, budgets, administration support, student dynamics, the stories kids bring, and the passion within a school or an institution. Having a reference work to bring the theory in *Kids These Days* to life would be critical. And then George said: "You need an educator to write it with you. Know any good ones?" Oh, did I! I'd met many as I toured schools throughout North America, and I knew instantly who I would partner with.

Long before I met George Couros, I knew Laurie McIntosh. She found me on Twitter, of all places. Twitter is a popular hangout for educators, who use it most productively to support each other in educhats (but also, unfortunately, to occasionally beat the shit out of each other's confidence). Before launching *Kids These Days*, I didn't even have a Twitter account, but as my work grew, I found that there was so much to learn from educators on this platform. So, I started an account and sent my first tweet about how I think educators can change the world. I got my first follower within thirty seconds—a self-proclaimed fan who had heard me speak many times! This was Laurie. Her profile picture was a shot of her and Ellen DeGeneres. Yes, *the* Ellen. Clearly, she was legit! Little did I know, Laurie was about to become one of my most influential teachers and the connector of all connectors in this tight-knit family of educator rock stars.

Laurie is the teacher I wish my kids had. That's how I judge teachers these days: Would I love for my babies to be influenced by this soul? Can I feel their passion? Because if I can't, I promise you, my kid won't. Do they have the capacity to be crazy (even quietly crazy)? Is there joy in their work? Every time I ran into Laurie over the following year—which seemed to be *a lot*—I became even more impressed with her passion, her crazy, and her desire to be better.

We were very clear when planning this book that two white women from small-town Alberta, Canada, wouldn't have all the answers or nearly the experience required to create an inclusive resource. So, we put out the call on social media and via our email lists for stories, insights, and what those of you who have lived this work thought others might need to know. Over the two years we worked on this book, we read, listened to, and cried over almost three hundred stories from educational assistants (EAs), teachers, administrators, bus drivers, and custodians across North America, all of which shaped this book that we're so honored you've decided to read. Some of the stories that took our breath away are included in the chapters to come. We hope you will feel the passion and wisdom in those we chose.

Now let's meet my friend, Laurie McIntosh.

Mrs. Mac of *The Ellen DeGeneres Show* Fame and a Dr. Jody Believer

When people ask me why I became a teacher, I'm never quite sure how to explain how I've gotten where I am today. Do I give the long, drawn-out version about not making the cut to get into the Faculty of Education, which led to an arts degree; an unexpected move back to my hometown; five years as an educational assistant; and trying again for my education degree on the heels of a traumatic relationship ending? Or do I give them the short version: I was called to this holy work. In so many ways, I'm a teacher because of all of it.

The immense sense of gratitude I have to be called "teacher" stretches down the long road it took to get here. This title was not obtained easily, and it's not one I take lightly. In fact, being "Mrs. Mac" defines me. This large piece of my identity reminds me (most days) that I matter and makes me feel like I am enough in this big world.

I find solace in knowing that every year I get the chance to reinvent myself, to "know better and do better," to paraphrase Maya Angelou. Throughout my life, I've had many opportunities to start again, but in 2015, I got a whole new shot at this Laurie McIntosh life. Let me set the stage. I was coming off my final maternity leave, struggling with the worst postpartum depression I had experienced with any of my three kids and feeling guilty that I needed to get back to work and become Mrs. Mac again instead of just Mama.

Seemingly out of nowhere, I got a call that January from the audience department of the *Ellen DeGeneres Show*. I had been randomly chosen to receive four tickets for a taping in February. As a huge Ellen fan, it was an incredible moment, but little did I know it would change the course of my life forever. (And to answer a few of the questions I get asked the most: 1. No, I don't know how I was chosen. 2. No, I did not know I would be *on* the show. 3. No, I can't get you tickets.)

I headed to Los Angeles the weekend of the show (coincidentally my birthday weekend!) with my family. Ellen and her team were amazing. Just closing my eyes and picturing the energy, light, and pure joy in that studio still gives me happy vibes. That would have been more than enough for me.

Then, at the last commercial break, my ultimate jam came on—"Ice Ice Baby." I know every word and even rapped it at my wedding. As the intro played, the hype man offered up the microphone to anyone who wanted to sing along. I don't think a mic has ever been pulled so aggressively out of that poor man's hand. (Sorry, Tom.) I rapped like my life depended on it. As I did, I looked up and saw Ellen. We locked eyes. She was clapping along and smiling. I inserted her name into the song. She slapped her knee. *She* saw me. My life was complete.

When the song ended and I sat back down, still on the "Ice Ice Baby" high, I heard my name. "Laurie! Come here, Laurie!" Ellen said, pointing at me. I don't remember running to her, but suddenly I was seated beside her. We played Heads Up!, and I crushed it, winning a trip to Vegas. As the theme music played, Ellen took my hands in hers, looked into my eyes, and said, "You were great! I loved your energy. I'd love to have you back someday!" I thought, *How sweet is she? I'm sure she says that to everyone.*

The next Friday, back at home and still riding the high from this once-in-a-lifetime experience, my phone rang, displaying "Burbank, CA" on the screen. An excited voice on the other end invited us to come back to LA that Sunday. Could we make it work? I felt it was probably inappropriate to yell, "FUCK YES!" into the phone, so I politely replied, "Of course we can!" We flew down and received some royal Ellen treatment, but my husband, Cody, and I had no clue what would happen next.

We ended up back in the audience. A woman sitting in front of us won ten thousand dollars. We cried. Ellen gave the entire audience tickets to the 12 Days of Giveaways shows. We sobbed. Then, a clip of my Heads Up! game played, and Ellen asked, "Laurie, can you come on stage?" I joined Ellen again, and we spoke about my family and being a teacher and about the Pay It Forward Wednesdays our family had taken part in.[1] How the hell did she know all this? For such a huge moment, I felt unusually calm and connected. She has that effect on people.

Not only did I go on to win a freaking car, but Ellen gave me all twelve days of the 12 Days of Giveaways, something she'd never done before. The value of all the gifts added up to hundreds of thousands of dollars. Through tears, I thanked her and said with conviction, "I will make you proud. And I swear I will spend the rest of my life paying this forward." She nodded with tears in her eyes and said, "You already have. And I know you will."

When we got back to the hotel, Cody looked at me and said, "This is the ultimate affirmation, Laurie. I hope you finally realize what a good person you are." He knew me and my struggles. He knew this was not what I believed about myself, but he sure hoped I would believe it now.

We flew home and went on a ten-month giving spree. We gave everything away, except for that car—which I still drive—and a trip to Hawaii that we took with our babies. We spoke to people to learn what they might need, and then we gave it to them. It was an incredible experience that brought us together as a family in the most amazing way.

When I tell this story, people always ask, "Why did she choose you?" Similar to the question of how I became a teacher, there are many versions I could give. The long, the short, the vulnerable. Ultimately, I don't really know—or want to know—why or how it happened. I like to think that I needed a reminder that connection, gratitude, positivity, and kindness are the keys to happiness. That I do enough, have enough, and am enough. It was the universe's way of re-teaching me some important lessons I had forgotten.

Outside of school, life after Ellen was filled with giving and connecting and gratitude. But life as Mrs. Mac was harder. I was in a place of doubt and worry, constantly tired and feeling overwhelmed. One particular Monday, I just knew: I was done. I was ready to make a career change. I was confident that the connections I had made in my community and the people I had surrounded myself with would guide me through to the next phase of my life. I finished the school year and secretly made a plan to move on.

In June, my friend Akemi messaged me: "Any chance you want to attend a full-day PD session in August?" *Nope. Not interested,* I thought. She didn't know I was struggling, and I wasn't ready to share. I decided, however, to take this as a sign to give it one more kick, and I replied, "I guess so." In response, she wrote: "Perfect! Have you heard of Dr. Jody Carrington? I will sign us up."

I had *not* heard of Dr. Jody Carrington, and I honestly was not excited to attend the session. In fact, I almost backed out that morning with a pretend illness. Turns out, you end up where you need to be. Jody began to speak, and I began to listen. I was hooked within five minutes. I realized there was no endgame. I needed to be surrounded by people who could remind me that this calling isn't about the methods we were taught but about the relationships we can form. That our kids deserve kind and supportive adults in their lives. That we need to take care of one another and relentlessly seek people who acknowledge the heart and soul needed if we are going to be effective in this holy work of teaching. You have to sit with the winners—those who also want to be great—if you want to change the conversation. On days when I feel defeated or frustrated, I still look back on the notes I took that day.

We need inspiration. For me, it was Ellen and Dr. Jody—two women to whom I owe some of my successes, my strengths, and my progress; women who gave me grace, acknowledgment, and a place to land. They did all of this with no intention to influence me specifically, but by the way they authentically show up in this world, they have led me to where I am: here, co-authoring this book, with the hope that our words will have the same effect for you.

How This Book Is Structured

My book *Kids These Days* was written as a theoretical platform for understanding kids. You do not need to have read it for this book to be helpful. *Teachers These Days* is the in-the-mess magic for those of you doing the sacred work, on the ground, of being a teacher. We want it to inspire teachers to incorporate relationship-focused, trauma-informed brilliance into every classroom that will have us.

Teachers These Days is organized to guide you through theory and then give you specific practical strategies. I will open each chapter with a psychological perspective about why we need to focus on relationships first—in any grade and on any campus. I'll talk about the developmental and neurological implications, and I'll infuse each chapter with the latest and greatest research so you know I'm not just making this shit up. (I'll make it much more fun than it sounds!)

Laurie will round out each chapter with the what and the how in the classroom, focusing on specific strategies for your students. We want to give you tangible things to take with you every day, and we also want *Teachers These Days* to serve as a reference anytime you veer away from your "why."

Every chapter will conclude with our favorite three, two, one: three things to try, two quotes to consider, and one question to answer (a summary strategy we learned from one of our favorite authors and culture creators, James Clear).[2] Then, in the conclusion, we'll wrap your heart back up and send you out into the world to do the work you were made for.

So, sweet teachers, I hope you will find the theory, stories, and strategies in these pages helpful and hopeful and that they will serve as a reminder every single day that every student, regardless of age, will show up in your classrooms seeking connection.

A Reconnection Revolution

Sweet mother of all that is holy, welcome, friends. I feel like we should be sitting down together—you, Laurie, and I—with big mugs of coffee near a sunny window, fixing to indulge in all the soul Laurie and I can muster. I'm hoping that, whatever stage you're at in your career, this very moment will mark a transition in your life as an educator and propel you into your next and best chapter.

Passion and Purpose

Passion rides shotgun to purpose. Full stop. Given that we're in the first chapter of this book, it might feel a bit early for a segue, but buckle up. Laurie and I are two of the most passionate people I know, so you're in for a wild ride. I wanted to write a whole book about passion because it's the thing I get asked about the most. Also, passion seems to be the one universal trait found in the happiest, most driven people I know. And we don't talk about it enough. So, let's start there.

Passion. Everyone wants it, but I don't think everyone understands how vitally important it is to fulfilling lives, careers, and relationships. Many people say to me: "I don't know what I'm passionate about anymore. How do I find my passion?"

As a fixer, I've often fallen into the trap of trying to fix some-one's desire to find their passion by suggesting strategies, usually ones related to happiness (because, clearly, happiness and passion go hand in hand). What will it take to get you to snap out of it and just be happy, dammit? When trying to blindly lead someone to their passion, I've asked dumb questions, with insinuating, underlying suggestions, like: Do you exercise? (Does it look like I exercise?) Are you drink-ing enough water? Do you journal? (Clearly, journaling is the way to clarity.) Each one of these questions is born from a sincere attempt to draw you down the path of happiness until you run smack into your passion—like it's a thing that's hiding in the bushes and you've just been too dumb to do all the things to see it.

Best-selling author Shawn Achor says that meaning and happiness cannot sustain themselves in isolation for long.[1] We often try to fix unhappiness, but rarely do we approach it through purpose. It feels hard. There's a lot to consider when we ask that huge question: Why am I on this planet? Turns out, however, the more I move into a place of finally loving what I do (most days), the more I realize how many others before me have journeyed on this quest to find their passion, too. They write about it (Simon Sinek), sing about it (Pink), talk about it (Oprah Winfrey). To get to your passion, you must first spend time with a less sexy question: What is your purpose? Show me a teacher who is clear on their purpose, and I will show you a teacher with passion.

Researchers who study passion have identified two types: har-monious passion and obsessive passion.[2] Harmonious passion is an internalization that leads individuals to engage in activities that bring them joy, whereas obsessive passion is an internalization of an activity that creates a pressure that ultimately thwarts healthy adaptation by causing negative affect and rigid persistence. When you find harmo-nious passion, you find psychological well-being that is often paired with inspiration, positivity, and empathy. It's not just something you love, but something that can define who you are and clarify what you stand for. Conversely, obsessive passion is often intrusive, paired with negative emotions, and can be debilitating and confining. Although it can also define who you are, an obsessive passion often limits your ability to see others' perspectives.[3]

For the sake of our work, let's focus on harmonious passion. When I meet the most inspiring and transformative teachers, they have a harmonious passion that even the maddest students or most crotchety parents can smell from the parking lot. I think it starts with clarity around this question: Why did you get into educating other people's children? Surprisingly, very few teachers have spent much time pondering this. (Let's be honest, the fact that you've found time to even read this book is a miracle.)

Now that we're in the space for miracles, when the stars align, it seems that those with the clearest sense of passion know these four things to be absolutely true. First, their life, at least to some degree, involves serving another. Second, that passion changes and morphs and waxes and wanes. Third, you don't find passion; it finds you. And, finally, passion is not an endgame; you can be clear about it one day and completely forget it the next day, but surrounding yourself with reminders in the tough moments is imperative.

Very few people whom I admire arrive at one passion in their life and stay there. At various stages, they have been passionate about different things. It isn't an end game; when you are driven by passion, it is often the driving force that keeps you in the game in the hardest chapters. This calling, this passion, will get you out of bed in the morning at the very least, and steal your sleep at its best.

Let's break it down. First, a big truth we'll talk a lot about: we are wired for connection. When we are at our best, we experience joy and are in relationship with others. Although there is peace in solitude, which can also allow for necessary growth and insight, we can rarely make sense of hard things alone for long. Serving another human, at its core, requires this thing called dual awareness. Dual awareness is the learned capacity of attending to one or more experiences simultaneously.[4,5] You first have to be aware that others, too, have a story.

A Ram Dass quote that I refer to every day hangs over my shoulder in my office. His profound words have become the foundation of so much we will talk about: "We are all here walking each other home." Read that again. That's it. That's all. At any given moment, in any given role, that is your job, my friends—walking each other home. I think that those words encapsulate a passion for each of us, particularly those of us who teach.

You have chosen a profession where you've decided to walk children, young people, learners, our next generation through their most formative years and developmental shifts. In K–12 education, you will see these children nearly every day for more waking hours than their primary caregivers will. In our post-secondary institutions, you will encounter students who are facing some of life's biggest lessons but don't yet have all the skills they need to confidently handle them. As a teacher, you will walk a lot of very impressionable humans home and often become an unforgettable part of their stories.

So, tell me, why did you get into education—as a bus driver, an educational assistant, a classroom teacher, professor, coach, custodian, librarian, administrator? You're a smart person, and at some point in your life, you made the decision—the conscious choice—to care for other people's children every day. Did you really think it through? Do you like lice? Do you like to clean up puke and poop? Do you like being told to fuck off on a weekly basis? Do you like being on the front lines in the middle of a global pandemic? Is your heart big enough to handle disclosures and heartbreaks? See what I mean? You could have been a barista! Or an accountant! But no—you decided to take on this sacred work of holding our most precious community commodity: our children. It's high risk with often low immediate reward. So, if there's anyone who needs to be clear on their purpose, dear one, it's you.

Since stories hold incredible power, let me tell you of one teacher who shared her why with me during a professional development session:

> In sixth grade, I was living in my third foster home. I'd come to school every day and spend some time standing

outside the staff room because it was the only place I heard laughter. Teachers would come in and out (often with smoke billowing behind them—this was a few years back). Of course, students weren't allowed in; it was sacred ground behind those doors. It sounded fun and connected. And I wanted to be a part of that family and be in a place every day where there was laughter. And that's why I'm here today, teaching in my eighteenth year. I know there are many babies, just like me, who need that joy and connection. Even on my worst days, I can give them that.

Even when you're just laughing in the hallway with a colleague, some student is watching, and what they're experiencing might be what they most need. So, if you haven't yet, stop what you're doing and answer this: Who inspired you? And why are you still committed to this profession? All bureaucratic bullshit aside, what does this work do for your soul?

I have been in educational facilities all over North America. I've taught university students. I've walked into schools where the principal, vice principal, and school counselor were in tears before I even took off my coat. I've felt the love, desperation, and exhaustion of so many of you. Those emotions and feelings of "not enough" are the fuel for my words. You're the reason that Laurie and I wrote this book. I started on this path of a reconnection revolution with my little team, inspired a lot by teachers, when we came to realize that the problem lies with teachers not knowing—because people rarely tell them— just how incredible they are. And I know this to be true: If teachers aren't OK, their students don't stand a chance.

Reconnection Revolution

Why, pray tell, do we need to be using words like revolution when talking about this reconnection thing? When Marti (my ride-or-die and now COO of Carrington & Company) came up with this word, "revolution," my first response was, "Hold up—this sounds like we're waging a war." I wasn't interested in being aggressive. I searched for something that would be a better fit, a softer, kinder, more inviting word. But the more time I've spent with educators, the more time I've spent with kids who are hurting, the more stories I've gathered about parents who question their competency, the more I've grown into my own skin as a parent, a wife, and a leader, the more I've come to know this: If we're going to leave a legacy to be proud of, it will require an effort that is revolutionary. It will need to be an effort of epic proportions that will involve one undeniable, unmistakable component: relentless passion for connection. There isn't a finish line. In fact, it's in the reconnection where the magic (and work) lies throughout the journey—which is why so many people struggle. And by the way, the people who need connection the most are often the hardest ones to give it to on any given day.

Our first stop, dear teachers, is to talk about purpose and passion. Without it, we won't ever get to the end of any school year—especially with curveballs like a pandemic thrown into the mix. We will be hard-pressed to find a healthy school culture if we don't focus on the passion of its individual members. Our hope is that we've got you thinking about yours. Your why. Your purpose on this planet. Another thing I know to be true in this whole purpose/passion quest is that drive is a common theme in purpose. So are energy, creativity, and imagination. These are the foundations of kindness, compassion, and empathy. And all of these things are intertwined and require emotional regulation.

Emotional Regulation

There is no more profound time in education than right now, in this emotionally charged, COVID-19 global epoch. The most important thing you will ever teach a child, inside or outside a classroom, is something called emotional regulation. The skill to regulate emotion is the foundation to every other skill that matters in a child's life, and understanding this concept will change the way you teach, lead, and love. I promise.

Emotional regulation, essentially, means how not to lose your friggin' mind. It's all about how you stay calm in times of distress or get back to calm after distress. Not a single one of us is born with the capacity to regulate emotion well. We have to be shown how to do it. Again and again and again and again. Newborns come into the world with three basic skills to help them communicate and regulate their needs: fight, flight, and freeze. For a baby, their primary mechanism to communicate emotional or physical distress is to cry (i.e., to lose their friggin' minds). Since most of us big people are hardwired for connection, we are pretty clear that our job is to soothe that baby. To walk them home. To help them make sense of the hard thing (the distress). Maybe not in those woo-woo terms exactly, but just watch any human being, regardless of race, religion, or cognitive capacity—if you place a crying baby in their arms, they will do their ever-best to soothe them.

When I, as a child psychologist, ask any parent what they want for their children, they answer with the one thing all of us want for our children and our students—for them to be happy. If I ask parents to expand on this, they will usually include some combination of three other things that they wish for their children: to do well in school, to make friends, and to give back to the world. Those things are so lovely. And so lofty. And so achievable *if*, and only if, the child has the capacity to regulate emotion. To stay calm in times of distress. To not lose their friggin' minds when they are challenged by a problem, person, or situation that they need to make sense of in order to return to a state of calm. To do all of those things (be happy, make friends, do well in school, and give back), they have to have access to kindness and empathy and have some capacity for dual awareness, all of which, you guessed it, require emotional regulation.

Here's the kicker. The only way—I repeat, the only way—you can learn emotional regulation is for somebody to show you how to do it. They can't tell you. You can't practice it when you're calm and hope to have access to it when you're distressed. Learning emotional regulation requires someone to show you how to do it, again and again, until you start to take on that skill yourself. There's no way around it, especially if you ever hope to pass that skill on to someone else. You can't give away something you've never received.

Now, if you ask any educator what they learned as they pursued their degree—in fact, if you review the teaching syllabi for most education degrees across this land—you will find a significant focus on literacy and numeracy. I promise you, however, that even with the finest pedagogy on your Flipgrid, you will not be able to teach anyone the things you want them to learn if they are emotionally dysregulated. I will expand more on the neurobiology of emotional regulation in chapter 2 when we talk all about the lid-flip. For now, just know that even adding the term "emotional regulation" to your teaching repertoire will expand your horizons and your teachability exponentially.

When we start to understand that a primary purpose of any teacher is to walk their students through hard things and that the only way they can teach curriculum is to regulate first, a clear purpose starts to emerge. If you are very good at regulating others, you will be one of the most influential teachers to those who need regulating. You have discovered the key: passion rides shotgun to purpose. Your purpose? Walking students home. Your passion? If you follow that purpose you will change the trajectory of a life, just by showing up and walking your students through hard things. Changing lives, as you do, is a passion that legacies are built on.

You will need purpose and passion most when you are faced with teaching emotional regulation. So just how do we do that in the trenches? How do we remember that we were once passionate when we are unappreciated, unsupported, or deemed nonessential? How do we remember when budget cuts come and report cards are overdue?

Here's where the beauty of this book comes in: I know the theory, but the practice will come from some of the best teachers out there. Let me pass it over to one of my favorite teachers who can tell you all she knows about losing it and then finding this crazy purpose/passion train again and again and again.

Where Are My Passionate Educators?

When I first heard Jody say, "Passion rides shotgun to purpose," I got goosebumps. As a teacher who has, sometimes, been fully aware and living my purpose and who, other times, has felt lost and confused about my why, suddenly the ups and downs of my teaching career made sense.

Here's what I've come to notice: The hard times? They all involved me ignoring my purpose, refusing to reflect on my why, or not living it like I knew I could. It wasn't those times of change and evolution that got me down—that was actually energizing and exciting!—it was the times when I flat out refused to follow my heart and lost my focus about serving others.

Let's be clear: your purpose and passion will not remain constants throughout your career or life. During those times when my purpose has been clear as day, I felt it was a privilege and a blessing to be a guide, an advocate, and a cheerleader to someone's everything. But during those times when I struggled to know my why and got lost and overwhelmed with all the responsibility that comes with being an educator and the judgment placed on me by myself and others (so often, to be honest, by the parents of the babes I was so committed to teaching), I was the one in need of a guide, an advocate, and a cheerleader to help keep me in the game.

Still other times, even if my why wasn't as clear as it could have been, I knew I was on a path of transformation and change through teaching. I was content with seeing where I ended up and how my passion reemerged. I remembered that purpose (just like connection with our learners) is not an endpoint; it's a constant journey of discovery and reflection.

As a brand-new, young teacher, my purpose had much to do with making a difference. I had been an educational assistant for five years, and with the amazing support of the teachers I worked with, I was confident that teaching was what I was called to do. I soaked in everything I could from every professional development session, staff meeting, and nerdy teacher talk. I learned so much from that incredible group. I felt like I needed those kids as much as they needed me. They fueled my passion. It was electric. Contagious. Energizing. I had made it to teacher status, and that pushed me to love our students and myself as hard as I could each day. I was serving us all. It was a wonderful place to be.

It turns out, however, that it doesn't take much to derail us. Sometimes, just one incident can make you question it all. When I was confronted with a difficult parent who tried to punch me in the mouth and lock me in a room during a parent–teacher interview, my purpose became muddled. It was still there, but I was too scared to live it. Was I truly making a difference if a parent wanted to physically assault me? I wanted to flee. I questioned everything and everyone around me and felt like there was no way I should continue on the teaching path. I felt worthless and terrified. The passion had disappeared, and I thought it was lost forever.

But as it often does with time, the tide of uncertainty receded. With some love from the sacred few who catch me when I'm falling, some reflection, and some therapy, I got back on the purpose/passion train. I decided that living on an island was no longer working. I thrived on connection and meeting new people, on telling my story and hearing the stories of others. I joined social media, which became my ticket to finding my purpose once again. It had nothing to do with likes and retweets and everything to do with connection, with conversations about the why with other educators who could empathize and uplift or challenge and question.

The Way to Passionate Classrooms Is You

Although I was now a connected educator in the Twitterverse, I felt a strong desire to move closer to the people who fueled my soul, so we packed up and moved our family four hundred kilometers away. Now, you want to get clear on what your passion might be in a hurry? Attend a job interview. I interviewed for a position, but despite being offered the job, I declined. Their purpose and mine were nothing alike. I would be climbing an uphill passion battle, which was in no way appealing to me. But after interviewing for my current district, I knew that my passions and theirs were a better fit and our intentions aligned. I knew they would love and support me and I'd be able to serve others.

I'm now convinced that my purpose involves creating a world I want to live in, focusing on our own classrooms and lecture halls. I want these to be places filled with kindness, grace, and gratitude where we celebrate one another and everyone feels included and valued. I feel immensely grateful that I get to do this every single day. Purpose and passion bring me back every time, helping me on this lifelong journey of reconnection as a teacher.

Finding Your Why

Although everything was unfamiliar and overwhelming when I joined my new district, I knew I could be myself and live my purpose—focusing on kindness, collaboration, and connection to our community. I could bring on the passion like never before. My new friend, Colleen, and I would check in with each other every morning to set our intention for the day. Usually, the conversation began like this: "So, what's your why today?" That question allowed us to reflect and challenge ourselves to commit to living our purpose in the classroom each day. It kept us accountable to ourselves and our learners. And the best part? I truly believe Colleen could tell you what my passion was before I could even get the words out of my mouth. She knows what drives me.

Here's my first practical strategy for anyone who is a teacher these days: find your own Colleen. This might be someone in the staff room at your own school or someone teaching the same course at another institution. Be brave enough to put your whys on the table with a trusted person and, every single day, make them a priority.

Whether you're finding your own purpose through reading, conversations with colleagues, a professional learning network on social media, your own reflection, therapy, or maybe even a ginormous career change, remember: When you are clear on your purpose, you will have the passion you need to be amazing. Being true to yourself and your purpose is always enough.

You Can't Tell 'Em, You Have to Show 'Em

I no longer panic when someone asks me to explain my why. Instead of answering with what I am, I answer with who I am. Although I may not always state it in the most eloquent way, I have a clear vision of my purpose as an educator and am able to verbalize why I do what I do. I can sum it up in three essential words: kindness, connection, and community. My purpose is to live and plan experiences of kindness, connection, and collaboration so that my learners leave kindergarten with a love of learning, asking questions and seeking the answers knowing they are leaders who matter in this world. Turns out, being able to tell someone why I am a teacher is never as powerful as when I show them—like when I actually show up for my colleagues, when I talk about students who've shaped me into the teacher I am, and when I honor the hardest parts of this work by sinking into the difficult conversations, resting, and coming back to my purpose again and again. On the days when I don't honor my purpose or use lessons or resources that fit my passion, I can feel it in my core, and I can often immediately see how it affects my students—who are always watching.

What We Do Is Amazing

Listen to me go, "What we do is amazing." I know I believe that about you and every teacher who has touched my life. But do we see it in ourselves? Do you really know how amazing you are?

Sadly, many of us don't. Heck! My freaking idol asked me to write a book with her, and my first thought was, *Well crap! She got it all wrong. There are so many amazing teachers out there . . .* Don't get me wrong, I have moments of amazingness, when my heart could burst with teacher pride and I believe I'm doing wonderful things. But they can be so fleeting. I suppose, when we literally make thousands of decisions a day, when we're unable to plan for everything thrown at us by the demands of the job, when we feel we've messed up someone's everything, we are bound to occasionally feel not so amazing.

What if instead of expecting greatness every moment of every day (and being disappointed when that impossibility is not achieved), we focused on what is right in front of us today? Instead of being all things to all people, what if our only job is to be the best we can be this year for these students? Whatever you have to give to them as you remember your why and show up with passion in your heart, that is enough. It simply has to be. I recognize that for some classes, some days, you will be more present, more passionate, more focused. Grace for the commitment to be there for other people's children is so important. You are already doing that every day. At the end of each and every year, I wonder if our only job could be to look back on a semester or a year and say, "I did the best I could with what I had for this particular group of learners, and it was enough." Period. Changing that language in my head and heart and measuring success in this way have made me feel (most days) like I am more successful than I've ever been, and I hope it will do the same for you, too.

Connection Seeking

Maintaining that feeling of confidence and sense of awe for what we do becomes especially hard when our kids are emotionally dysregulated. We take it personally. If we only were good enough, if we just gave them the attention they're seeking, they wouldn't lose their minds. But, in the same way we can reframe our idea of what makes a good teacher, we can also change the language surrounding dysregulation.

Dr. Jody's attention-seeking versus connection-seeking words hit a chord with so many of us for a reason. We've all heard the attention-seeking comment used about a challenging child. And, chances are, we have felt overwhelmed by such a child's behavior. Let me tell you about a time I did.

Kindergarten, also known as The Land of Dysregulation, is where so many of our youngest babes begin the journey of figuring themselves out. When I heard Dr. Jody's description of the lid-flip, it changed my life and revolutionized our classroom (and I don't use that word lightly). I went from being a teacher who believed many things I don't want to admit on paper to a teacher who finally understood that a child's only job is to flip their lid and get it back on. And I had to be the person to show (not tell!) them how to do that over and over and over again.

I had been a self-proclaimed kindergarten lid-flipping master for some time when a new child entered our classroom. This child flipped their lid like I had never seen and lost their ever-loving mind twenty, thirty, forty times a day. I was stunned. And exhausted. I watched as other children became fearful of the flips. I watched as other adults rolled their eyes as if to say, "There they go again." I watched as this child cried and screamed and scratched and fought their way through each day. In my utter exhaustion, I, too, started thinking they were just looking for attention. Ugh. Gross. I was mad because my ego was hurt, and an educator with a hurt ego is not someone I want to be around, never mind learn from.

I knew nothing about this particular learner's history, but I went into investigative mode. Was I missing something? I requested files and started tracking triggers. I convinced myself that if I could just figure out the pattern, I would have this licked. I focused on methods instead of our relationship. I documented behaviors, made tally charts, put extra strategies into their instructional support plan (ISP), removed the rest of the class when they flipped, and, and, and . . .

Any guesses how that went for me? Terribly. With a capital T. I was perplexed as to why I wasn't making any progress. Then, after a particularly difficult day, I did some Dr. Jody note reading and realized yet another shift in my mindset had to happen and a change in my language and priorities were necessary for me to help this child.

I went back to the basics, remembering first and foremost that it was their job to flip their lid, that they were in the fight of their life. It didn't matter that I didn't know the whole story; frankly, it wasn't mine to know. I kept reminding myself that just like I never gave up on my own children when they cried/screamed/lost their minds as infants, I could not give up on this learner, either. This was not attention-seeking behavior. This child needed connection like no other I had encountered. This child was not there to be fixed, but to be seen, heard, and valued. I reminded myself with every lid-flip that I was given a gift to help this child get it back online. Again. And again. And again. Every lid-flip is an incredible opportunity to connect and learn from one another. It was a constant challenge to keep in mind that to self-regulate you must have connection. I needed to connect. Stat.

I had to start by examining my own triggers. What did I do after that careful reflection? I rocked. I hummed. I often didn't use words. I took deep breaths. I gave space but never left them alone. I tried in every way I could to show them that the world is safe and not scary. That they could depend on me and would not have to navigate this alone. I was relentlessly there (almost) every time they flipped their lid. I learned their pet's name and their middle name. I met their eyes. I used their name, and they started to use mine. I made sure not to avoid the lid-flips (that always got me in trouble) and to connect before we repaired and directed them onward. I needed to remember that there was a difference between calm and quiet and that this child needed me to help them find the calm. And slowly and surely as the weeks went by, things got better for both of us.

This is not the part of the story where I say something ridiculous like, "And they never became dysregulated again!" Nope. We had insane amounts of success, but that success still came with lid-flips. Every. Single. Day. A day without a lid-flip does not equal success. That is not the end goal. So, how do I know the year was still a success?

On the last day of kindergarten, this particular child came to me and said, "You must be sad it is the last day of school today." I explained that I was used to having to say goodbye but that, yes, a part of me would be sad our year together was over. They nodded, smiled, looked me in the eye and said, "Yeah, but now that I am leaving for grade one, you are going to have to find a new favorite kid."

A lid-flip is not a mistake. It is a wonderful opportunity to learn and connect with our kids. Connection and attachment are our educator superpowers. This is what makes us amazing. Not that we prevent lid-flips and that magical, little, self-regulated angels float around us all day. Not at all. Lid-flips equate to learning for all involved—including those who are watching. What makes us amazing is that we come back every day ready to show our kids that we will be there for them. That they are not problems but opportunities who are worth it.[6] That they are part of our purpose and fuel our passion in so many ways.

Wrapping Up and Moving On

Friends, it is time for the reconnection revolution. We are the ones we've been waiting for. Connection—because we're wired for it—is often the easy part. It is the reconnection—to our why, our health, our people, our breath—that will allow us to serve this profession and the students and families who seek to learn and be better year after year.

Reconnection is a necessary skill when we step into the hard things like grief and trauma. We leave you with a summary our friend James Clear uses that we call our "Three, Two, One."

Three things to try

- Write down one or two teachers who you will connect with (by text, phone, email) in the next few days who will remind you (and you will remind them) why you do this work, especially on the tough days.

- Consider a time when you felt the most conviction in your career, when you felt you were making a difference. Where were you? Who did you work with? Remember what it felt like to be that person, and know that if it doesn't feel that way now, that teacher is still in there.

- Think about those students whose lives you've changed. Keep a visual reminder of them close. Write their initials on a sticky note. Keep their photos on your desk. Gather their drawings and notes in a folder or box, or scrapbook that shit. If you ever doubt your impact, look at these things and know you've made a difference.

Two quotes to consider

"Connection is the easy part. Reconnection to the things you were once connected to but have lost is the tougher part. Connecting to the people, places, and passions that matter to you—that's where the magic lies, and the real work to finding your purpose begins." —Dr. Jody Carrington

"There is no passion to be found playing small—in settling for a life that is less than the one you are capable of living." —Nelson Mandela

One question to answer

- What, or who, inspired you to become a teacher and, maybe even more important, what, or who, inspires you to stay in this incredibly life-changing profession?

Taming the Crazy by Getting Crazy

"**C**razy" is a pretty risky word for a psychologist to open with. It's definitely an attention-grabbing word. I trace my use of it to the quote by psychologist and Head Start cofounder Urie Bronfenbrenner that tells us the one thing every kid needs to develop in a healthy way: "Somebody's got to be crazy about that kid. That's number one. First, last, and always."[1,2]

I love that damn quote and that dead guy for saying those words. Friends, this isn't anything new or groundbreaking. It's the truth, as simple as it is complex, and it's something I take very seriously. When we understand that all any kid needs is someone to be truly crazy about them, then everything, and I mean everything, will change. Of course, the kids who need this most are the ones who are hardest to give it to.

As so many of us can attest, having a theoretical parenting or teaching practice does not necessarily speak to how we show up in every moment of every day. Even with creativity, insight, and a large dose of grace, we will fuck it up. What we must do is make sure the base we return to when things fall off the rails is solid and empirically supported; this is critical to running any successful classroom, organization, or relationship, period. That base, particularly when serving developing humans, needs to be two things: relationship-focused and trauma-informed.

Now those two phrases get thrown around a lot; however, I want to break them down here and expand on them in the chapters that follow to explain just what it means to be relationship-focused and trauma-informed. To get really fancy, I will outline the significance of considering attachment and developmental research as you plan for your classroom and your curriculum so that your teaching is built on the solidest of foundations. (It'll be more exciting than it sounds, I promise.)

This chapter is about the biggest lessons I've learned as a psychologist. It's the necessary, underlying philosophical practice that I think needs to be universal. We often talk about strategies or approaches, but rarely do we talk about what we fundamentally believe to be true as we respond to and incorporate our strategies. Any successful organization, business, or family is clear on what they fundamentally believe. The mission statement withstands the storms. The foundation of any successful endeavor is the people who make up that organization and, more important, how they interact with each other. The importance of focusing on relationships first is very hard to operationalize in a numbered format, which is why I think it becomes so difficult to accomplish, particularly when we get scared or overwhelmed. We want a plan, a policy to fall back on. The hard part is that the healthiest teams know you need those things in place for success, but they must be built on a foundation that is solid and meaningful first.

Let's start with this: a teacher's greatest superpower has very little to do with pedagogy or practice. You know this. It's kindness. Even as I've sat with people in prison or with parents whose kids have been apprehended, when I am regulated and have access to empathy, I can understand behavior. That doesn't mean I condone, support, or believe in that particular behavior necessarily, but empathy provides me with so many resources to promote connection and the possibility for collaboration with another person. I don't think it's kindness we lack. I think it's our access to it (in the most difficult times) that causes problems.

How do we lose access to our kindness? When we stop seeing it as our biggest strength, we also stop seeing it in others. We stop valuing its importance. We stop operating from a place of connection and grace, which, in turn, results in systems, relationships, classrooms, and cultures operating in a place of disconnect and defensive armor. In an effort to fix things, we create programs and responses that are structured and planned, and often in that state, we forget that none of our plans work without the relationship in place. Even if these plans do sometimes work in the short term, it's the long game we're playing, friends. We often forget about kindness in the moment and become focused instead on extinguishing the troublesome behavior. Getting rid of unwanted or inappropriate actions is how behaviorism was born, and it's critical we understand it and its purpose.

Behaviorism 101

The premise of strict behaviorism is reinforcing the good stuff and punishing the bad stuff. In theory, and indeed in practice, this seems to work. It worked for rats and pigeons, so, obviously, it should work for children. The outcome, the behavior, is often what we measure. Rarely do we look at how we got there.

Just two generations ago, we lived in smaller homes, taught in smaller schools, and spent more time in community and far less time on technology. We had more proximity to one another, and by virtue of this fact, there were more opportunities to interact. This interaction—physical, face-to-face connection—is critical for the development of emotional regulation skills. So much of what we teach our children is nonverbal. So much of how we communicate the skill of emotional regulation comes from being in proximity to one another and rarely from the words we speak. Because we took this proximity as a given, we failed to realize how critical it was to the effectiveness that appeared to come from a strict behavioral approach.

Today, as we raise, teach, lead, and love our students, what has shifted significantly is our proximity to them. Admittedly, other components have also changed in just two generations, and proximity also gave way to disconnection and abuse that often wasn't talked about like it is today. As the pandemic has reminded us, our need to not only look at but truly see one another cannot be replicated with automated connections or replaced with busyness. We are wired for physical connection, and I think the effect this loss of proximity has had on our ability to connect and teach emotional regulation and worthiness has been profound.

We start to assume that kids are lazier, more disrespectful, and not as motivated as they were in the good old days. There is no evidence, however, to suggest this is true. In fact, as I've said many times, inspired by the great psychologist and founder of the Self-Regulation Institute, Dr. Stuart Shanker,[3] I've assessed and treated more than a thousand kids in this country and I've never, not one time, met a bad kid. The majority of children I have worked with over the years struggled with one common thing: regulating their emotions in times of distress.

We've Come a Long Way, Baby: Behaviorism to Relationship

I've talked about the virtues of a relationship-focused, trauma-informed practice for so long now that sometimes I'm a little taken aback by the vastly different theoretical approaches that still inform the culture in any given school. And not just schools on different sides of the planet. I'm talking about schools located across the street from one another. Why is that? Do you just get lucky sometimes and end up in the right place? What is the secret sauce in getting to be on "that team" where most everyone just gets it? Where kids aren't feared and staff rooms aren't avoided?

There's little bureaucratic standard of practice regarding how any given district is structured. Sometimes there are three superintendents, sometimes one. Sometimes there are assistant superintendents. Sometimes there's a director of learning, a director of innovation, and a director of cultural diversity. Sometimes no one does this work, and sometimes one person does all three jobs. From an organizational perspective, I can imagine it would be difficult to measure the most effective structure if there isn't a school division that operates all schools in the same fashion. This often results in far less collaboration between districts or institutions and way more competition for who is ahead of the curve or who has engaged in a particular program that might serve their kids and families better. It makes sense, I suppose, because in most structures there is competition for the students. Frequently, funding depends on enrollment—bums in seats. If you're fighting for limited resources, you no doubt want to be the best. As an avid sports enthusiast and self-proclaimed hockey legend, I have a huge appreciation for healthy competition—its purpose is to advance the field or organization and honor mutually held values. It's a fine line, though, when we step into this place of scarcity and fear that can create a tendency to diminish others in an effort to win validation (or funding!).

I completely understand that every single school division on the planet has different geographical make-ups, cultural and economic diversity, and access to resources that can dictate these differences, and many are at the whim of local government funding. However, I think the structure of a school or district is not nearly as important as the underlying philosophy of those who serve in our educational institutions.

That lesson became clear to me when I started my very first job as a registered clinical psychologist, working on a locked inpatient unit for kids. There was the obvious need for structure and protocol and behavioral plans to manage the very problematic behavior these babes had been admitted for. When rules were broken, a common consequence was a twenty-four-hour loss of privilege (LOP). "Can I take this kid off the unit for an activity?" "Nope, he's on an LOP." It was a standard of practice, applied across the board, regardless of story, situation, or circumstance. The intention was brilliant. There needs to be structure in place so kids learn limits and boundaries. They need to know they are safe and when (not if) they push those limits and boundaries, they will be steered back to safety. And they probably won't like it. It was clear, from my naive perspective at least, that the intention behind LOP was to shift behavior, to punish the bad stuff in hope that kids would learn to be kind, respectful, and appreciative, so that when they were released back into the "real world" they would have learned the importance of consequences and breaking rules and they would be nice.

I understood it. I still do. And here's the issue with a government-issued standard of practice from a behavioral perspective: It works. It's effective—remarkably effective, to be honest. If you have a big enough stick, turns out, you can get almost anyone to do almost anything. The kicker, however, is what you're left with: disconnection. It's an issue that the forefathers of psychology were not particularly interested in when they first developed this theory. They were jacked to discover that when you rewarded a rat with a pellet, it would keep pushing the lever. When you shocked the rat, it would avoid the lever. Well hot damn, they thought, we need to do this with kids! So, they did. So, we did. So, we still do. Here's why . . .

We put a very high emphasis in this culture on emotional regulation, that sacred state when people use their words, remember their manners, and don't lose their friggin' minds, especially in public. We are fans of regulated kids. We've always been fans of calm over chaos. Here's the tricky thing, though: the chaos is necessary to learn the calm. You must first be dysregulated in order to learn how to regulate. The lesson comes in the walking home—getting from the dysregulated chaos to the calm. It's in that journey that the answer lies, and it's in that journey that we have very few lesson plans. Taking stuff away or punishing or shaming someone will not create emotional regulation skills. It may result in behavioral change, but it will never create humans who can pass on the skills we want them to learn and absorb.

For me, two basic understandings, neither of which we are born with, facilitate this process. I was shown how to do them by some remarkable teachers, ones probably just like you. These two skills have connection as their foundation, and there are two important components to effectively teaching them. The first is the mechanics behind emotional regulation, and the second is how you get there. If there's anything you can tuck into your teaching tool kit to forever change your career, it's these. Drum roll, please . . . let me introduce the lid-flip and the light-up.

The Lid-Flip

I didn't learn about the lid-flip in grad school. In fact, I don't ever recall understanding the neurological underpinnings of behavior until I saw psychiatrist Dan Siegel explain it in a video.[4] He oversimplifies the most complex organ in our body in a way that helps us understand its mechanics. Simply consider the brain as two parts: the upstairs and the downstairs brain.[5]

It's Siegel's visual that gets me every time, so play along at home. Make a fist with your thumb tucked in underneath your fingers. If you hold it up in front of you right now, you will be looking at a hand model of your brain. It's about the same size as the brain currently located in your head. As you look at your fist-brain, imagine that your arm represents your spinal cord and your wrist represents your brain stem. That brain stem is the most primitive part of your brain and houses some critical basic functioning, like control of your heartbeat and your breathing. As you'll see, your brain stem wrist is connected to your thumb. If you flip your fingers up right now, it will reveal that precious little thumb tucked very safely inside your brain. Your thumb represents your limbic system. That seemingly inconsequential thumb houses the three basic emotional regulation responses that all mammals have: fight, flight, and freeze. These primitive responses pay no mind to race, religion, gender identity, or socioeconomic status. If you're a mammal, you got these three for free. This is how infants communicate before their ability to form language.

Now fold your four fingers back over your thumb. These represent your prefrontal cortex. The prefrontal cortex is what sets us humans apart from most other species. It's where everything you've ever learned in your life lives, like how to drive, how to dance, what your best friend's middle name is, and what year you got married. It's also where the best of you lives: kindness, compassion, and empathy. Think about those four fingers as a lid. Siegel says when that lid is on, you have access to everything you've ever been taught in your life (access to the prefrontal cortex). So, for example, when you look at your own child (if you have one) making an appropriate choice or decision, calm and open, their lid is on. In those moments, they have access to everything you, and everyone else, have taught them.

Now, have you ever heard the expression, "He's flipped his lid," or said something like, "I don't even know who you are anymore"? Have you ever flipped your own, personal lid, doing and saying things that, in the moment, felt pretty friggin' good but, later, when your prefrontal cortex settled back into place, left you feeling guilt, shame, and remorse? It's a universal human process. You cannot teach anyone anything when their lid is flipped. A limbic system (a flipped lid) alone cannot learn. The teaching comes through the easing of that lid back into place. Some call this process co-regulation.[6] You can slam a lid back on using fear or threats (and sometimes this is necessary), but that strategy results in no learning of emotional regulation. All that is being taught is that if you scare someone enough, they will comply. And compliance is very different from growth or respect.

Here's the other thing that lives in the prefrontal cortex: your capacity to repair post-flip. The apology thing also wasn't pre-programmed in us before we were born. Someone has to show you how to repair in order for you to be able to do it yourself and then show another person. If you have never been apologized to, if others have rarely stayed calm in the midst of your distress, you will have little tolerance for the distress of others. All you will do in response to distress is what you've experienced: flip your lid.

Here's why, holy rollers, you teachers are so critical. In the run of a school day, how often do you observe your students flipping their lids? How often have you walked someone else's child through a lid-flip? How many times have you gotten a kid back on track by showing them how to do it? Those experiences are not just lessons; they are the moments when neural pathways are created—neural pathways that kids will eventually be able to access when no one is there to help them. We are all wired for connection, remember? We can't learn these things in isolation. Now here's the trick: Remember the effectiveness of behaviorism with rats and pigeons? If I punish them enough, the unwanted behavior stops. The same is true with children. If you take the things they love away from them enough times, the undesired behavior may stop; however, it's not replaced with kindness or connection. You have built no skill in emotional regulation. You have, essentially, taught them what they already know: only fight or flight works with other humans.

When that prefrontal cortex is flipped, you will only observe the most primitive behaviors. In the biggest lid-flips, kids (and adults) lose their words and resources. They may be able to communicate with grunts or hisses (my personal favorite when my kids lose their minds); however, they no longer have access to language. And if they can't produce language, they can't process it. So, no matter how extensively you lecture or remind them to use their words, it will never work. Not because you're not right, but because they (their limbic system) can't, in that moment, process what you're saying. In fact, never in the history of telling someone to calm down has "calm down" ever worked. If you question this, try it on your spouse or teaching partner. How do they respond?

There is one very important caveat to this whole thing, and that is when violence or a significant threat is present. Then, all bets are off. This is what the brilliant Circle of Security theorists call a "take charge moment."[7] Your greatest task becomes keeping them safe. For example, when the bell rings and you have thirty-four kids to corral into the classroom, this isn't the time to regulate emotion if two babes are pushing each other. You take charge. "Hey. Enough. You over here. You here." That is where kids learn when they've gone too far. But when they're upset and don't have access to their prefrontal cortex, we are hoping yours is still intact, so that you can walk them home.

Speaking of which, what happens when their lid is flipped and yours is, too? How does this typically turn out? You guessed it: not awesome. Which is primarily why we're writing this book: If you're OK, if you understand the prime importance of keeping your lid on, then and only then can you serve, teach, lead, or love to the best of your capacity. If your lid is flipped, these babes don't stand a chance. The other (life-saving) kicker that I'll say here, also a lesson I learned from the Circle of Security clinicians, is that we as adults only need to get this emotional regulation thing right about 30 percent of the time to teach it well enough.[8] You read that right. We can screw this shit up a lot. And we do. Because we're tired. And we have a lot of things to manage. Most every person who reads these words will doubt their ability, at some point, to parent, teach, or serve kids and families. We will all flip our lids. Our only job is to remember just how critical it is to simply walk kids through their distress whenever possible.

The other thing that I think is critically important, which I didn't spend nearly enough time talking about in *Kids These Days*, is what happens when you don't keep your lid on, when you lose it. The art of repair is, in fact, one of your most significant skills, so much so that we decided it deserved its own chapter. Hence, you will read more about repair (and what happens when you don't make repairs) in chapter 7. For now, let's focus on how we get to putting the lid back on, which is often rooted in our second life-changing concept: the light-up.

The Light-Up

Lighting up is all about the joy you have in connection to another human being. It doesn't have to be big or loud; it can be subtle and quiet. But when you know the language of someone's light-up, you know when they're doing it because of you. And you will discover the power of it.

Let me walk you through an obvious light-up. Think of the airport reunion of two young lovers who haven't seen each other in months and have been counting the minutes until they will be in each other's arms. (Whoa, what just happened there? That was some serious Nora Roberts shit. I might have to make my next book a romance novel.) Or when a grandbaby hasn't seen their grandparent in months and they run to them with open arms. The response? That's a light-up. A response that is heart-filling, full of warmth and joy. Often it involves some air being sucked in, eyes widening, and hugging. The telltale signs that a light-up has occurred are that there will be joy and often laughter. You know you matter. There's no hiding it.

Conversely, think of the relationship you have with someone who is a little less demonstrative. Take my husband, for example. He's a farmer. He loves cows—so much so that he has a PhD in ruminant nutrition. He's one of the most brilliant men I've ever met—with the least demonstrative disposition on the planet. When his bride calls (who, can I just say, is basically a rock-star lighter-upper), he regularly answers the phone with nothing more than a "ha." Not even a full "hey"; just "ha." It's uncanny. And here's the deal: he has always been the rock for me. (Let's be clear, not The Rock, who I'm guessing is a little more demonstrative in his light-up, which I would be open to testing if the fates allowed.) Anyway, I can tell you that our children have completely different experiences in the light-up from their mom and dad. When Aaron lights up with our children, it's not loud. It's a nod or a smile where the lines beside his eyes get deeper, and they just know. They also never question their father's sincerity. The quiet ones sometimes require more work, but when you get the light-up, you know it's genuine.

The point is, dear ones, it's not *how* you do it, it's *if* you do it that matters. Please know this: you don't need to show up any differently than you do right now for the people you love, lead, and teach. You don't need to be louder or quieter. All they need is you and your light-up that's just for them. It's a superpower that is perhaps the most critical, underused precursor to any teaching. And the hard part about it is, once again, the people who need it the most are the hardest to give it to.

Let me tell you a bit more about that. You know who it's easiest to light up around? The kids who are regulated. The ones who can keep their lids on. The ones who can use their words, get their assignments done, ask the impressive questions. We like those ones best because we put a high emphasis on compliance in our culture. That's the thing with the light-up: it's usually a thing we save for the people we like the most. But, if you start giving it away more often, particularly when it's difficult to do so, I promise you it will snowball, spread, and carry a shock value that changes lives.

Here's what I mean. Think of a colleague (current or former) who you just can't deal with most of the time. The one who for some (likely obvious) reason makes you want to lose your mind. Maybe they're the one who can't wait for retirement (and they've been teaching for six months) or the one who always has something to complain about. Or maybe it's the one who's always so damn happy you're convinced they have edibles stashed in their desk. Either way—got them in your head? Now, how easy is it to light up for them? They may rarely receive it, not just from you but also from others who respond in a similar fashion. It's not uncommon, in fact, that a light-up is a foreign response to some people (big or small); they're surprised (and sometimes suspicious) when someone is excited to see them. In fact, imagine what that person would do if you came into the building on the next school day and genuinely lit up when you saw them.

Here's another thing you should know about the light-up: Typically, we're better at it when we have no skin in the game, which means our access to vulnerability and kindness is readily available—like when we're trying to impress someone. Think of a first date. You generally wouldn't begin one by saying "ha," and if you did, you likely wouldn't get a second. The people we love the most are often suspicious when we're kind.

And one last light-up lesson. Light-ups don't always have to happen in the moment. The power to give away the light-up even years after a meeting can be just as powerful.

Rhonda's Story

I became a teacher because of Mrs. Tatlow, my grade one teacher. She was kind and had the best light-up. As a woman in my forties, it seems ridiculous to write now that one of my biggest influences in this world of education happened in grade one, but it reminds me of the impact that educators have at every age and just how long-lasting those interactions can be. On my fortieth birthday, the strangest thing happened. My phone rang, and an oddly familiar voice on the other end said, "I'm calling to wish you a happy birthday. It's Mrs. Tatlow." I was stunned and moved to tears. I asked her how on Earth she remembered my birthday. Mrs. Tatlow explained that she had written down the birthdays of all her students and she makes it her mission to track them down on their fortieth birthdays and remind them of the impact they made on her. This woman was my inspiration. And now she is my hero.

The moral of this sweet story, dear ones, is that it's never too late for a light-up. You are woven into so many stories and I promise you, even after thirty-six years, so many of your students will never forget you.

So, there you have it, friends, two little concepts that are absolutely critical. Keep this gentle reminder close: your job is to get flipped lids back on, and your clearest, most direct pathway to de-flipping any lid will first, last, and always involve the light-up. Even a spark is enough to light up a whole room. Whatever you got, on any given day, is more than enough.

Let's Talk Strategy

I'll toss this important section to Laurie. We asked so many of you on the frontlines to tell us how you actually, in the moment, manage the lid-flips, the dysregulated babes. And many of you said it comes down to the light-up.

Boo to Behaviorism

I was an educational assistant before I became a teacher. During those precious years in that role, I realized something very important: you don't need a classroom to be a teacher. Some of the best school cultures are centered around remembering that schools were built for children to learn in, not for adults to have jobs in. When I reflect on my career and the many stories I've heard from teachers just like you, most memories have to do with either lid-flips or light-ups. Those are the lessons that stay with us, change us, and make us who we are.

The biggest lid-flipper I ever worked with taught me more than I ever taught him. My greatest memory of him was one fine day when he screamed at me to "SHUT UP!" in the middle of a quiet, productive, early elementary math class. (For the record, I wasn't even talking.) I immediately removed him from the room, and we went on a "walk and talk." We walked. I talked. He was quiet. I would have even said calm. Look at me go with my effective strategies! I had won. I had talked enough, said all the words he needed to hear to teach him to never again tell me to shut up.

We were about to return to class, cool as cucumbers and ready to learn, when I saw him counting on his fingers and smiling. My response? "Oh good! It looks like you're ready to get back to math now." He smiled an even bigger smile and turned my way holding up two fingers.

"I have two words for you. Shut. Up." He laughed. Excuse me, young man? Oh no, you didn't! I upped the ante. "Well now, it looks like you haven't learned your lesson. I guess we need a little visit to the office as you're obviously *not* ready for math. And while we're at it? You miss recess today!" He laughed. Shit. I knew I was in trouble.

He now had four fingers up. He said, "I have some math for *you*. Two plus two is four." He very slowly continued. "So, now I have four words for you. Shut. The. Fuck. Up."

Boom.

The reason this story has stayed with me is that, first off, it's hilarious. Although I was frustrated with the clear failure of my strategies, as soon as he said those four words, I was caught so off guard that I laughed. And, immediately? He laughed, too. The energy changed. I'd let my authoritarian guard down, and he was thrilled. I'd become more human to him. Although I was still irked, the laugh started the process of regulation and reconnection for both of us.

Second, this episode stuck with me because it gave me a huge realization about forcing students into compliance versus authentically working through lid-flips. Normally, I would have beaten myself up for that unexpected giggle and told myself I was condoning his poor choices. But something changed that day. I realized I wasn't condoning the behavior. I knew the swearing would need to be addressed, but it hit me that it wasn't the time to talk about it. Yet. It wasn't *if* I would address it, it was *when*.

The truth was, he actually did need me to shut up and probably needed something to eat or drink so he could process and get himself regulated again. And to be honest? So did I. A dysregulated adult cannot regulate a dysregulated child. That boy changed my belief that there was a timeline to dealing with behaviors. Immediate discussion and consequences had been my jam. I didn't know any better at the time. But now I do. And I'm so grateful he taught me this lesson.

Rosalie, a student services coordinator, won me over with her story of humor as the best intervention.

Rosalie's Story

I'm someone who loves to work with the honeys who struggle. One day, a young boy sought refuge in my classroom after his teacher sent him to "go out and calm down." He came in cursing, refusing to do his work, saying, "I hate school! I hate everything about this!" After waiting quietly, I calmly said, "How do you think I feel? I don't even like kids." He stopped, jerked his head to the side, surprised, and started to laugh! The most beautiful laugh! He didn't need to hear me lecture about how his behavior was inappropriate, and he most definitely didn't need to hear about making the proper choices. He needed to connect. He needed to start over and do so in a dignified way. He needed to know someone was still there when he was flipping his lid and to know we weren't that different. He needed to share some joy.

In situations like these, reverting to rewards, punishments, and behaviorism makes sense in our minds, especially when we feel angry, tired, frustrated, or lost. It gives us an immediate sense of control over the situation. But these lessons don't stick. They create a situation for our learners to demonstrate compliance, and compliance is always temporary. The only way to teach them differently is to model what we want.[9] Over and over and over again. Regulation is the goal here. Not compliance.

Treasure Boxes or Sticker Charts, Anyone?

Anybody got themselves a class treasure box? I learned in university that the treasure box would be one of my most essential and necessary classroom management tools. Treasure boxes, sticker reward charts, clip charts, ticks on the whiteboard—ways to track and reward good behavior (aka compliance)—are based on the psychology of behaviorism. They can lead to embarrassment and shame for many of our learners. Clinical psychologist Ross Greene says, "Stop giving stickers, taking away recess or suspending them. These kids want to behave."[10] Managing a classroom is so much more than behavioral management. I want to be a teacher students tell their kids about someday. The one who saw them for who they are and who valued and honored them in a dignified way. Not a teacher who relied on prizes, trinkets, and stickers to gain a false sense of relationships based on compliance and fear. Token systems based on behaviorism are rooted in our own biases and created expectations. They have no place in the classroom.

Making a shift from rule-enforcer to needs-noticer was a big one. Sometimes, especially when I'm not taking care of my own needs, I easily revert back to the old, gross behaviorism ways. It's how I know I'm off track. I often get asked, "But if you don't use a clip chart, what do you use?" I use relationship-building. And humor. And interest in their interests. And face-to-face connection. Most of all, I use my two superpowers: walking them through the lid-flips and giving them the light-ups.

Getting Their Lids Back On

It's so critically important to remember that lid-flips are not mistakes; they are learning opportunities. Constantly working to avoid them is problematic because it's exhausting (and impossible) and because it's through the chaos that we learn the calm.

You will notice that this section of strategies mentions nothing about identifying triggers and eliminating them from a learner's world in order to avoid lid-flips. It also doesn't involve making lists of motivators to trick them out of having lid-flips. Instead, we'll focus on strategies to help put lids back on when the flips happen and recognize that we cannot keep kids in a perpetual emotionally regulated state.

Trigger Storm

We all come into a classroom community with our own stories and identities. With that, we come with our own triggers. My triggers tend to be noise related: a loud cry, a fierce whine, a fist slam. Identifying my own triggers and learning how to acknowledge them and how to recognize my own unhealthy reactions to them has served to de-escalate more situations than I could possibly count.

One night while making supper, I snapped. I yelled at my kids and my husband who were being "TOO DAMN LOUD AS I AM TRYING TO COOK YOU A NICE FREAKING DINNER!" As we sat down to eat, I apologized for yelling. I explained that they had done nothing wrong. It was in fact my low noise tolerance that had me frustrated and led to the rage. My nine-year-old said, "Wow, Mom. Hashtag triggered." Sigh. Thanks, son. But funnily enough, I often approach a flipped lid situation with those words in my head: "Are you hashtag 'triggered' here or is this actually something that needs to be addressed?" Learning to acknowledge our own triggers is an essential first step in determining whether a child has flipped their lid or whether it's you who is about to flip yours.

A Shift in Language

One of the most effective strategies I have found for dealing with a flipped lid (and for keeping my own damn lid on) happens well before the lid even starts to flip. Before the grunts, furrowed brows, and the hint that something is brewing, a change in language needs to happen. I have to move from thinking about the students as *my* learners to seeing them as *our* learners. These children do not belong to you or me. They are someone's everything. This change in perspective, as witnessed by the change in language, is essential to building a community of caring adults around those we serve.

I first learned about this important shift in language from the incredible educator, speaker, and author A. J. Juliani.[11] You see, when I continuously call them "my" kids (as loving, caring, and kind as that can be), I'm subconsciously putting pressure on myself to be this child's everything. So, as my lid begins to flip (because that's bound to happen), I start to feel like a failure. I start to think that I can't handle him/her/them/this situation/this job. I start to feel more and more alone. And we were never meant to do any of this critical work in isolation.

Using "our" purposefully reminds us that we work together. No one can do this job alone. No one. We need each other, and our learners need all of us to be on their team, showing them the way with the best we've got on any given day.

You Don't Pick Them, They Pick You

One of the hardest lessons I've had to learn and relearn over the past fourteen years is that kids choose their anchors. We cannot designate ourselves as someone's person. They choose us. Or maybe they don't choose us. And, either way, it has to be OK.

When we can let go of our egos and allow other adults in our school communities to connect with kids in our classes, every child's needs can be met. If I claim a student as mine and don't foster multiple connections with the people they choose, I'm doing them a huge disservice. When they flip their lids and I say things like, "I got this!" or "I know what I'm doing here, thank you very much" or "Do *not* go and get Mrs. S. She was last year's teacher!" none of these help; they harm. And, even worse, there's a good chance that they escalate matters.

Need some alternatives? Try these for size:

- Who can help me get this kid's lid back on?
- Am I contributing to the chaos or the calm?
- Who/what can help us get to the calm?
- What am I missing right now? Who can help me see it?

I keep a running record of who each learners' "person" is in our school. If it isn't me, I need to know who they have built a connection with. And, again, I need to be OK with it. It might be Sergeant Steve (the SRO who constantly just pops in), Mrs. Chan (the best custodian on the planet), Mrs. Cormican (who teaches next door and has the patience of a saint), Mrs. Schmold (who gives our students the first light-up of the day), Mrs. C (who will sing to them in her rose gold microphone), or any other adult in our building—our kids choose their person. I don't. When I figure out who that is, I write it down to remind me that I'm not alone. And, when shit really hits the fan and I just can't anymore? I know who to call. And, if they do not have a person? That is terribly concerning. If I'm not the person for them, I need to let go of the ego and find them one. Stat.

You never know who they will choose for their person. The key is recognizing their choice. For Jennifer's student, the division's electrician, Mr. Darrell, is one of his favorites.

Jennifer's Story

> Mr. Darrell is kind, patient, and will do anything to support our student, Charlie. Charlie lights up every time Mr. Darrell arrives at our building, and Mr. Darrell lights up when he sees him. Mr. Darrell told us that whenever he is having a rough day, he will pop by our school to see our little guy!

Relationships know no hierarchy. Regardless of titles, you are currently surrounded by experts in relationships. Be open to the incredible possibilities each adult in your building holds. And maybe, just like Nikki, you will find them right in your room ready and willing to jump in.

Nikki's Story

One year I was gifted an amazing kindergarten class. My classroom had extremely diverse needs. I was also gifted with four educational assistants to help support those exceptional students. I was a seasoned teacher at this point but didn't have the skill set to handle all of these diverse needs.

After my first half day, I felt defeated and wondered if I could handle this plus four other adults in the room. I cried hard. When I was done, I realized that I didn't need to "handle" the four adults in the room. I was *blessed* with four amazing individuals who had years of experience working with students one on one. I knew I needed to push my ego aside and rely on that knowledge and experience to build our classroom community. I trusted them. They had the freedom to make the choices they knew were the best for all the children in the room. We created an amazing, inclusive family where everyone had an anchor and belonged.

Time after Time

In the midst of these lid-flips, one of the most powerful tools you have in your pocket is time. I know so many of us want to argue with, "But there's never enough time in my day," and you're right. It certainly feels like we go from one thing to another all day long.

Although we have the best intentions as we guide a student through the process of emotional regulation, if we cannot slow things down, we will fail. More than that, we might make the situation even worse. I get it, our days are built on strict timetables. But taking the time to work through a lid-flip is critically important. It's not a process I can rush no matter how damn hard I try. Think for a moment how empowered you feel when someone says, "It's OK. Take your time." Taking the necessary time to ensure our students' lids are back on and that they're not just quiet but calm is an important part of getting through this together.

Show, Don't Tell; Listen, Don't Talk

There's so much power in showing someone how to regulate. Matching a lid-flip with an equal or even more intense flipped lid isn't effective. I'm reminded of this constantly as a mom when I scream at my yelling kids, "WOULD YOU STOP YELLING ALREADY?!" It's never quite been effective for me. Shocking, right?

Remember, if a child doesn't have the capacity to produce language, they cannot process language. Spitting, grunting, hissing babes have no capacity to hear what we're saying regardless of what we say or how we say it. I constantly need to remind myself that there's no fixing with words in these times (which is hard for this teacher's brain to comprehend). Deep breaths, head nods, and time are all I've got.

Once they scream, "What the hell, McIntosh?!" (a favorite way one of our little guys demonstrated he was able to produce language again after a lid-flip), I know we are back in business and words can be introduced again. (Remind me of that the next time you see me trying to talk someone through a lid-flip, would ya?)

Not just hearing but listening is key. Lorrie, an educational assistant, told us a story about a grade six student whose father died by suicide. Upon his return to school, this student refused to talk to anyone. Except for her.

Lorrie's Story

I had no training, no education, no suicide prevention courses to give me guidance. I thought, "What if I wreck this kid?" My principal assured me that the child had asked for me and only me, and if nothing else, I could just listen—so that's what I did. I walked into the room where he sat alone, and his eyes lit up and he hugged me. For hours, he kept crying and asking, "Why?" I just said, "We may never know that answer, bud. I am so sorry." That was over twenty years ago, and he still hugs me when he sees me.

Rest assured we'll talk more about this whole lid-flip phenomenon as we go on. Practice makes progress, folks. We will not get this done perfectly. We're going to screw it up. Constantly. There are going to be times you'll have to tap out. And that's OK. That does not demonstrate failure. It shows you are learning. And that's the name of this game.

It's Not the Method, It's the Light-Up

If you've ever had the pleasure of meeting Dr. Jody in person, you will have seen and felt the enormous power of a light-up. This girl can do it like no other. No matter if it's the first time you meet or the millionth, the eye contact, the squeal, that sharp breath in, the smile. It makes you feel seen, heard, and loved to the umpteenth degree.

That's not to say that this is the only way to light up for someone. After meeting Dr. Jody, I'd think to myself, "Oh! So that's how you light up? I'm going to need some practice!" Wrong. My light-up doesn't resemble hers, but that doesn't mean it's wrong or even less effective. A light-up, done authentically, in your own way is powerful no matter what it looks like.

Much like Dr. Jody, I have a husband whose light-up doesn't look like my light-up, but Cody's has changed and evolved throughout our years together. His light-up for our kids is different than his light-up for me. And I love that. That light-up is special to me and me alone. When I see it? I'm energized, full of hope, and feel loved. But I've also been told that my light-up is too much. And Cody has been told that his isn't enough. I call bullshit. No one gets to tell you how you light up. Your own unique light-up is an incredibly powerful tool as a spouse, educator, and human on this planet.

Lighting up takes courage because it means becoming vulnerable. Vulnerable enough to show happiness, lean into joy, and say, "You matter to me." When I let out, "I'm so happy to see you!" with my wide eyes and toothy smile, it's the epitome of me showing that I really do care about you. That, my friends, takes courage.

So, when we talk about strategies for lighting up, we don't tell you what your light-up needs to look like. You know within you if your light-up is real. And those who are blessed enough to receive it? They will know, too.

Meet Them in the Hallway

A 2018 study conducted with middle school students showed that when teachers started class by welcoming students at the door, academic engagement increased by 20 percent and disruptive behavior decreased by 9 percent—potentially adding "an additional hour of engagement over the course of a five-hour instructional day."[12] Seriously?! Can you believe that? Furthermore, these researchers suggest that "teachers who spend time on the front end to implement strategies such as the PGD [positive greetings at the door] will eventually save more time on the back end by spending less time reacting to problem behavior and more time on instruction." Low cost, high yield? Count me in.

Meet them at the door and show them with your eyes, smile, posture, and body language that you truly are happy to see them. That the class wouldn't be the same if they weren't there. That they matter. We're all asking one fundamental question as we walk through this life: Am I worth it? With your light-up, leave them with no doubt that they truly are worth it to you.

Up the Ante

Want to up the ante with your light-up? Throw in a compliment! If you struggle with giving and getting them, that's OK. It just takes practice. Start small with something like, "I'm happy you're here," or "Nice hoodie," and move on to things like, "I just wanted to thank you for that awesome thing in class yesterday." You can even move on to more complex compliments and affirmations until you are at a Mr. Rogers level: "You've made this day a special day by just being you. There's no person in the whole world like you, and I like you just the way you are." How's that for a compliment?!

Another tip is that you don't have to be physically present to light up for someone. Notes of appreciation, either given in person or tucked away for someone to find, phone calls to thank someone for a job well done, or a virtual class shout-out over Zoom (if a learner is comfortable) are all ways to show our gratitude for this time we get to spend with them and for all the effort they put forth.

When I think about getting a random "Thanks for this awesome thing you did at work" Post-it Note on my laptop from a friend, I instantly light up. I want to work harder and be my best me. In fact, a Harvard University study "found that when people were reminded of their best work, as if they were hearing their own eulogies, they had more creativity and less stress."[13] The eulogy part may be a bit morbid, but let's focus on the legacy-you're-leaving thing.

Find ways to hand out compliments and affirmations like freaking candy. Don't hold back. Don't wait until it is too late. Normalize thanking learners and your colleagues for their hard work and showing gratitude for all they do. This reminds them that they matter to you.

Lighting Up Means Showing Up

When they need someone to eat lunch with or play basketball with at recess, when they need someone to listen to their new mix tape (that's still a thing right?!) or read their latest poem, when they need to tell someone all about the latest TikTok, just show up. Heck! You might even get a birthday party invite or a hockey game schedule. If you're comfortable, show up.

Roxanne's Story

Last year I decided I needed to figure out what these kids were all about. I posted on our class bulletin board a "What are you doing?" section where students could share their school activities and any extracurricular events they participated in. I told them my goal for the remainder of the year was to spend some time with each and every one of them *outside* of school.

Jay couldn't afford to participate in extracurricular anything. One recess in early April, I overheard him talking about going to see if the local skatepark was snow-free. After school I headed over there. A handful of boys were there, and he was one of them. Remembering the gigantic smile that spread across his face still brings me goosebumps. He bolted toward me and gave me the most amazing hug. He asked me what I was doing there, and I told him I came to see him skate. I sat there for over an hour while he showed me every trick he knew. His excitement was through the roof. I laughed, cringed when he wiped out, and cried when he came to hug me for a second time just before he left. Jay is now in grade eight. I have supported him throughout the last few years. My door is always open, and the best part is, he knows it.

Give It Away

Lighting up for a caregiver is an incredible way to build relationships. As is so often the case, those who are the hardest to give it to need it the most. Connecting with the families we serve by phone or email or in person has incredible effects.

I remember calling a mom of a learner who challenged us daily. I wanted to share some good news about her baby. She answered the phone with, "And what the fuck do you want, Teacher?" No hello. Just that. I was caught so off guard that it was hard to recover. "Hey there. Sorry to bother you if this is a bad time. I was just calling to thank your daughter for her help today. A friend got hurt on the playground, and she swooped right in to help. She showed kindness and empathy and courage, and I just needed to say thank you."

Silence. Then, "Cool. Thanks." And a hang up.

But, guess what? My relationship with that little one was influenced that day. Mom showed up at lunch the following week. She didn't speak a word to me, but I heard her say to her daughter, "So, can you show me the friend you helped? I just want to make sure she is OK."

And the next week at dismissal, I overheard her tell a dad in the hallway, "I hated school when I was her age, but my kid? She likes it. So, I guess that's good." And when she came for parent–teacher interviews? She sat and listened to all of the positive things I had to say about her incredible girl, then said, "Yeah, but now tell me the bad stuff. That's what my teacher used to do." When I said, "I got nothing. She's wonderful, and I am blessed to spend this time with her," she buried her head in her hands and cried.

Beat them to the punch. Don't call only to share the negatives. Call, first, to share what you love about their kid. Then, when you need that caregiver on your side to help remedy something, you'll have a much better chance of getting to their head because you have made a connection to their heart.

My friend Barbara, a school counselor, tells this story anytime she hears the word "light-up."

Barbara's Story

My great-aunt Norma modeled the light-up. Instead of entering a room with, "Here I am," she exuded enthusiasm and said, "There you are!" She made me feel like I was her absolute favorite for the entire time I was in her presence. Turns out, she shared the gift of her light-up with more than just me, as evidenced by what happened at her funeral. When the pastor asked the congregation to stand if they were Norma's favorite, nearly the entire congregation stood up. After all, she had been a first- and second-grade teacher for fifty years and had taught almost every child in our rural area. They had come back to pay their respects and thank the woman who told them with her eyes, her smile, her unconditional love, and her loving kindness that she saw them.

Be someone's Aunt Norma. See them with a "There you are," and then hear them. It's a legacy in the making.

Wrapping Up and Moving On

Drop those shoulders, friends. So far, we've set the stage for what's important, and it's everything you're already good at. You don't need anything more than what you've got right now: a heart to influence humans who want to learn. This chapter was all about getting to those hearts, especially the ones who need it most. It's something that is so easy to know in theory and sometimes so hard to do in practice. Let's leave you with a few final notes of promise in our three, two, one.

Three things to try

- Light it up. Choose one person today you cross paths with and genuinely light up when you see them. Notice what happens.

- Give away some positivity today: a smile, a coffee card, a compliment. Do it on purpose and notice how just by giving it away, you can change the trajectory of a life. You do it all the time without knowing. Start taking stock of just how influential you are to so many people every single day.

- When someone (anyone) you're teaching is dysregulated and their lid is flipped, try offering them a drink or a snack before using words to figure out what is making them so frustrated or upset.

Two quotes to consider

"When they're acknowledged, they will rise." —Dr. Jody Carrington

"If you could only sense how important you are to the lives of those you meet; how important you can be to people you can never even dream of. There is something of yourself that you leave at every meeting with another person." —Fred Rogers

One question to answer

- Think about a time you've been most influential in your role as a teacher. What was it about that student that made that interaction such a success?

3

Kids These Days: How We See Them

A babe can show up (entirely) differently in two different settings. This tells us that we can see the very same kid and have completely different experiences with them. Ain't that the truth? Ever have a kid in your classroom who was off-the-walls, life-suckingly disrespectful? Then, you'd go into the staff room, start to talk about how exhausting this little muffin is, and some (damn) colleague would say, "Oh, I love that sweet boy. He never acts that way in my class," and you would (hypothetically, of course) want to throat punch her? Or better yet, when the kid gets pulled out for therapy and this lovely therapist, who this kid adores and only seemingly plays Uno with for one hour a week, gets all that kid's respect and compliance, while you get nothing but swearing and defiance? Why and how is this possible?!

One thing I've learned is that kids often look very different in person than they do on their diagnostic profile or in their education file. I've gone back and forth on the idea of reviewing a kid's history before assessing them versus allowing them to teach me who they are in our meetings and then reading their file. I have come to the conclusion that there isn't a right way to best prepare to understand or assess a kid, but I do know there are often many sides to a story (just like the ones you and I bring into work every single day). Objects in the mirror are not as they appear—at first glance anyway.

A Typical Consult

Some of my favorite moments in my practice come in the form of consults. See, I love the hitters, the kickers, and the biters. If there is some stealing and lying and bomb-drawing in a kid's profile, I'm your girl. There have been more than a few times when I've seen an education file the size of the King James Bible sitting on a table, surrounded by a few exhausted and sometimes pissed-off teachers, EAs, and a principal. I can usually predict what that education file will hold: at least one or two psychoeducational assessments, an occupational therapy consult, a speech-language consult, a few codes, and a whole whack of behavioral support plans, where a lot of "motivators" and "triggers" are circled and highlighted. There's generally also been some discussion about the significant concern that the staff has for this child, including all of the behavioral presentations that are "attention-seeking" or "manipulative." Sometimes the words "sociopathic" or "bipolar" are used. On more than one occasion, I've closed the file, looked at these amazing souls desperate to assist this babe in her learning, and asked, "Who can tell me her middle name?" Or I might ask, "What level is she on in Fortnite?" or "When was the last time she saw her mama?" When I have a staff member who can answer those questions, the education file tends to shrink faster than with any behavioral support plan I've ever seen.

Whether you're assessing a kid in a clinical context or teaching them in a classroom, having more pieces of their story will almost always add more fuel to an empathy fire. See, we're wired to make quick decisions about people based on their behavior—it's not only primitive but, in many cases, protective. What allows us to soften or to sink into empathy for another, where we can temporarily suspend judgment and have greater access to kindness and compassion, is when we have insight into why people show up as they do. We don't necessarily condone or even support the behavior, but the shift in the question from "What's wrong with you?" to "What happened to you?" can change everything.[1] That question is often the impetus for empathy.

This significant yet often overlooked fact is a critical concept for any clinician or educator. Making time to learn the context or the reason why someone shows up the way they do will result in the most drastic response shifts to even the most difficult behavioral presentations. One of my favorite lines on this topic is from my friend, the activist Jesse Lipscombe, who said, "Change moves at the speed of empathy."[2]

Born with and Acquired

Before we step into the meaning behind behavior, I want to review a simple little strategy I used at Alberta Children's Hospital when I was trying to understand a kid's presentation. I would take what I knew about their diagnostic profile or behavioral presentation and separate it into two categories: born with and acquired. Think about a student who struggles significantly in your class or maybe one you've been worried about. Just using what you know about that kid in this moment, consider any diagnoses they have been formally given (like attention deficit hyperactivity disorder [ADHD], oppositional defiant disorder [ODD], or a learning disability) and any other concerning behaviors that you have noted or that might be documented on an individual education plan (IEP). Next think about what was known at the moment of their birth, when someone laid that baby into the arms of a caregiver for the first time. What did they have on board from a neurological perspective? What challenges may they have already been faced with? These are the pieces of their story that we can assume they were born with. Kids are born with the things that affect their brain (neurological conditions) like learning disabilities, fetal alcohol spectrum disorder, autism spectrum disorder, and ADHD. You don't acquire those things; they come with your genetic makeup or your prenatal experience. Other presentations that get a little less clear are things like anxiety and depression; they come with a genetic predisposition, and it's often safe to assume that for more severe anxiety (e.g., when kids meet criteria for obsessive-compulsive disorder or the rare diagnosis of pediatric bipolar disorder), there's a neurological component from birth. We will talk about the more frequent experience of acquiring anxiety or depression below.

Conversely, many of the things we see in kids in the classroom developed in response to things they have experienced throughout their life, so we can consider these presentations acquired. As we talked about earlier, kids are not born with the ability to regulate emotion; they must be repeatedly shown how to calm down before they can get better at mastering this skill called regulation. One example is the diagnostic label ODD, from the *Diagnostic and Statistical Manual of Mental Disorders* (DSM-5), which is the bible of psychiatric disorders. Oppositional defiant disorder requires kids to display a pattern of at least four symptoms "for at least six months" from a list of symptoms that includes an "angry and irritable mood, argumentative and defiant behavior, and vindictiveness."[3] I don't think I've met many kids who haven't gone through at least a phase where they would solidly meet all criteria; however, kids who have experienced significantly difficult histories *should* present that way. Does it make it acceptable? Absolutely not. Does it make it understandable and hence that much easier to hold space for and make a plan about? Absolutely.

Kids are not born with ODD; in fact, ODD is a descriptor for children who have significant and long-lasting difficulty regulating emotion. Further, when the behavioral presentation continues to worsen or when they start to harm others or themselves, we then graduate into the diagnostic category of conduct disorder (CD). A kid will meet criteria for a CD if they violate the rights of others (e.g., aggression toward people or animals) and violate societal norms (e.g., destruction of property, theft, or frequent truancy).

Both ODD and CD are simply descriptors of a behavioral presentation, not neurological conditions. (You can't have them both at the same time, by the way.) Furthermore, personality disorders, which should rarely be used as descriptors for children but sometimes are, are also not neurological conditions but acquired. Often, many presentations of personality are developed in response to or exacerbated by experiences in the child's life, and many of these can be identified as traumatic. (More on that in the next chapter.)

Where this gets a little dicey is when we consider diagnoses like anxiety and depression. Many babes you teach will experience anxiety. So do many adults. By basic definition, anxiety is your body's natural response to stress. It's normal. We want kids to be anxious sometimes, dysregulated and scared, particularly when they step into new spaces—physical, emotional, or intellectual newness should reasonably come with some anxiety. Overcoming anxiety, or calming through a stressful period, is necessary in order to learn that we can, indeed, do hard things in life. Experiencing challenging situations and coming out the other side serves to reduce anxiety and increase confidence. You can't tell a kid how to overcome a hard thing; you have to show them and, often, walk them through it so they can learn the skills to eventually do it on their own. I hate this about so many things in life, but the truth is, there's no way around it: you have to go through it.

I like to think of anxiety and depression on a continuum. (A supervisor in grad school once explained this beautifully to me, and I never forgot it.) Think about anxiety as the very overactive, busy, hyped-up response to something that scares you. If you're able to work through, face, or overcome that fear, anxiety dissipates. If you do not, eventually, that anxiety can exacerbate and avoidance of a feared situation allows it to grow. Some people stay in this fearful state and develop a clinical anxiety, which essentially means it interferes with day-to-day functioning. For other people, if this persists, the management of all of that hyped-up emotion becomes exhausting and starts to fade into something that looks a bit more like depression. Your body gets too tired from constantly having to hold it all, so there is a give-up factor that can take over—an exhaustion that is like walking through wet sand while wearing a suit of armor. This can become depression.

It's extremely helpful to distinguish what a student is born with and what they have acquired, particularly when you're considering the behavior they bring into your classroom. It can sometimes help us understand that we're not wrong in identifying the behavior (e.g., lying or stealing), but when we start to understand why they've developed those coping strategies, the answers of how to address it become so much clearer. Let's go there next, to those attention-seeking, manipulative liars. Those are my favorites.

Attention Seeking Is Connection Seeking

The reason people—little and big—get emotionally dysregulated is to get attention. Read that again if you have to. Kids are, indeed, more often than not, trying to get our attention. Not because they're "needy" or "clingy," per se. We're wired to connect to others around us when things get too difficult or too exciting. Kids often lose their minds in order to get some help handling emotions they're not able to make sense of alone. I've heard this phrase so often in my career: "That kid is so attention-seeking." And truer words were never spoken. I promise you this, however: if you make one subtle shift from thinking of a child as attention-seeking to connection-seeking, the story of their behavior will also change and, often, so will your response to that behavior.

Connecting to others in order to survive and grow is the primary job of all tiny humans. In fact, we never outgrow this. I can bet that today you've sought attention from someone to help you make sense of something. For example, if a kid challenges us or we get some upsetting news, we tend to seek out someone to bounce it off of or to help us manage the load. We were never meant to walk this planet alone. The more reliable, safe, and predictable the responses from others become, the more you will seek their support to help you through the hard things. If you've been taught that others cannot be trusted, for a litany of reasons or, even worse, that they're harmful or scary or unpredictable, you stop seeking them out. The seeking out is a good thing.

In addition to our experiences, temperament also plays a role. I feel like I'm the boss of this because I had two tiny humans come out of my uterus on the exact same day and they couldn't be more different people. There is, by the way, evidence that both experiences and temperament play into the presentation of every child[4]; however, I am quite comfortable saying that the response to how kids show up is much more predictive of who they turn out to be than what they were born with.

Culture and Bias: What We Didn't Know We Needed to Know

Explicitly weaving culture and bias into how we understand children is necessary. It's always been necessary. In my position of white privilege, I used to consider myself aware, but let me be completely honest, I wasn't (and still ain't) anywhere near "woke." As Layla F. Saad explains in her groundbreaking book *Me and White Supremacy*: "You cannot dismantle what you cannot see. You cannot challenge what you don't understand."[5] I can't believe how much I don't know, but because it's sacredly important, I'll start with the little I've learned so far.

A bias is a tendency, inclination, or prejudice toward or against something or someone.[6] Biases are often based on stereotypes rather than actual knowledge of an individual or circumstance. Whether positive or negative, such cognitive shortcuts can result in prejudgments that lead to rash decisions or discriminatory practices. More specifically, an implicit bias is any unconsciously held set of associations or beliefs about a social group that can result in the attribution of certain qualities to all people who belong to or identify with that group. Implicit biases are the product of learned associations and social conditioning, likely from the people we grew up with. They're formed and maybe informed by our respective trauma histories.[7]

I want to make it explicitly clear that this material is not exhaustive and should only be considered the start of a conversation. In fact, it's so much easier not to start it. Because then you don't risk missing anything. Or messing it up. Or getting into a debate that's not yours. I'm starting to understand that what you permit, you promote. Silence breeds permission. And equity and justice matter more than any of the teachings in this book. If there's no acknowledgment of what your students, your staff, and each of us bring to the table, it will be that much harder (if not impossible) to properly serve the kids who sit in front of you or the families who love them. My intention here isn't to speak for anyone, particularly those whose insights, writings, teachings, and stories are far more credible than this white girl's attempt. Listening, listening, listening (that's the critical part), learning, speaking, and showing solidarity in our actions, posts, and the people we are honored to sit with, in that order, will remain the focus for the rest of my days.

Showing Up in the Classroom

I'll turn it over to Laurie to talk about the first and necessary step of making space for the stories your students bring into the classroom, the behaviors used to play them out, and how our biases as teachers sometimes show up.

Unpack with the Best

I, too, have never been more aware of my own biases and feel like I've just scratched the surface. I've learned especially from two amazing educators, Naomi O'Brien and LaNesha Tabb, whose incredible book, *Unpack Your Impact,*[8] has greatly influenced the way I think about students. I had no idea how much bias I had against the students who didn't show up the way I thought they should. I didn't want to have these biases, so I did my best to pretend they weren't there. Turns out, the acknowledgment that they exist is sometimes the hardest but most significant part in the journey. And of course, it's not a one-shot deal. O'Brien and Tabb have taught me that this is a process. The work is never done. That was a huge wake-up call.

The bulletin boards I put up, the lessons I deliver, the books I choose to provide and to read, the activities I plan, the manner in which I deliver them, my assessment practices: all of these need to be reflected upon and checked for biases. Listen, it's humbling to say that it's taken me until now to feel like I am even aware of my biases (let alone tending to them), but I'm a billion percent confident in saying that this work is more than worth it. I'm grateful to have strong leaders who've taught me the value in being vulnerable enough to speak the words, "I have a bias." We all do. For me, racial bias is admittedly where I need significant work.

Reflecting on our own biases and adapting the classroom environment to those we serve is essential to connecting with kids. It's critical that we change to meet the needs and stories of all our students and not the other way around. We serve them. It's not their job to serve us. Although we should expect more responsibility if we teach older students, college kids who are often in the middle of so many transitions have stories that need to be heard and appreciated, too. Biases run strong at every age.

Lynn's Story

Ty, a connection seeker, was late every single day. One day we were walking to the library and I said, "How can I help you be on time tomorrow?"

I ignorantly thought I'd help him develop a schedule or teach him how to set an alarm on his phone. Instead, he waited for all the other students to pass and stood with me, alone in the hall. Ty said, "My mom works the night shift. She sleeps until the minute I need to be driven to school. I get myself and my baby sister up and feed us both. It's never my fault. I'm doing the best I can."

It felt like I had just been slapped in the face. I was harshly reminded of the reality that some kids face. From that day on, I never asked a kid why they were late. I started saying, "Thanks for making it in today. I'm so happy to see you!" This small change led to a world of difference.

What can you change about your own practices to adapt to those you serve? Action based on honest reflections is merely the first step in this very important process. Ask yourself the hard questions and lean into the answers. To overcome, we must see all of it—the kids, the answers, the questions—closer up than we ever have before.

Start Fresh

Every year, the same situation plays out in schools everywhere. Some crotchety old teacher spends the entire year complaining they've got "the worst class ever." This is the year that "the kids have never been so lazy, disorganized, or rude." I've been "warned" about just how bad it will be when I get them next year. June comes and they push the transition plans your way and wish you a sarcastic "good luck." Maybe you spend your summer reflecting. Are they really *that* bad?

I'm convinced that misery does, indeed, love miserable company. It also appears that long-standing biases are difficult to change. Sometimes it's so hard not to be influenced by first impressions or others' opinions about a kid, but I remain shocked at how the same kid can show up entirely different, not only from year to year, but from class to class. There's so much merit to giving ourselves permission to start with a clean slate at the beginning of a new year, a new class, or even the next day following a blowout. What we expect from a student usually comes to fruition. We might as well aim high.

I love this story from Darren, a teacher who tells us how important it is to be brave enough to ignore the negative claims made by the stories that precede a student. One child's grade two teacher had a warning for Darren: "You do not want this kid in your class. He's the most miserable little SOB that you will ever meet. He'll be in the office every day."

Darren's Story

He was a very small, spiky-haired bundle of energy. Both parents often smelled of alcohol when they came to pick him up. He was friendly and liked to chat. When issues arose, I found that talking to him and working through the cause of a meltdown was easier than sending him to the office. That little boy didn't need a teacher on him every moment of the day expecting him to get it all right. He needed someone to hold space, someone he could just talk to. I know I don't get it right all the time—I'm a teacher and human—but for that student that year, I feel like I got it right.

Years later, I happen to look out the window of my office and see a truck parking. A young man gets out and begins walking across the grass toward our school entrance. Then, I hear a voice at my door. "Is Mr. P available?" There, before me, was this very same kid who "would be the most miserable little SOB that you would ever teach," now eighteen, who drove out just to see me. His visit still brings me to tears. This is why I do what I do. I do it because you never know when you might be the right person for the right kid at the right time.

I'm eternally grateful for second chances; I've needed more than my fair share. For many of our learners, the situation is the same—they need that teacher who will seek to find the good. Kids deserve second chances. And third chances. And hundredth chances. No matter how they show up. Even the one who screamed about what a shitty teacher I am today? Even her. Especially her.

Starting fresh doesn't mean waiting for a new day, week, or year to begin. It means making a split-second decision to acknowledge our own hurt, name our feelings, and choose to give another chance. And almost always, it's preceded by a deep breath. Just for kicks, fill those lungs right now, dear teacher. There are many kids I wish I'd given the benefit of the doubt. Usually, in the moment, I don't have the resources, but I use that deep breath to ground myself as often as I can muster it.

I spend an entire year with other people's children. Giving up on them or treating them a certain way based on a bad day or another teacher's opinion is not an option. Instead, I will be brave and courageous enough to say: "What you did hurt me. It was not OK. But I choose to try again." And, to be fair, I only hope they'll extend the same grace to me when I screw things up.

Gail—a teacher who was "very pregnant"—was struggling with a boy who had been dealt a tough hand.

Gail's Story

He said, "I hope your baby dies." Those words brought back memories of my second baby being air-lifted away by ambulance and, with them, so much pain. I left the class, marched to the principal's office, and said, "That's it! I am never coming back here again."

In a meeting with the student the following day, he told me: "You have two kids, and you're about to have number three, and you love them all. I want you to feel sad like I do when no one loves me and is always mad at me."

All behavior comes from somewhere. The good, the bad, the ugly. After my baby was born, I showed up at this student's soccer game to cheer him on. I wasn't even sure if he noticed I was there. He was good, and I found a grant to help get him proper soccer gear. The following September, I came back as a sub, and when I stepped into the building, I saw him coming straight for me from down the hall, arms wide open. He asked if I remembered the time I came to his game and updated me on soccer. I could see the connection. I will never forget him.

When we speak of this kind of grace and forgiveness in our communities, here's the most important question: Are you giving yourself the same grace, understanding, and forgiveness you extend to others? You, amazing one, are where all the power lies. At the top of that lecture hall when you teach five hundred or sitting criss-cross applesauce with a snotty, sobbing little muffin, it is all important, hard work.

What Do You *Really* Know?

When I meet someone for the first time, there are a few things I hope they say as they walk away from our conversation. Maybe something like, "She's so kind and authentic," or "She's a great listener," or, since we're big dreamers here, "I like the way I felt around her." Does it always work out this way? The answer, of course, is no. I'm not for everyone, and neither are you. And that's OK. Really, it is.

Those are merely the first things I hope people feel meeting me— your list may look drastically different—but there are so many things I hope they learn as our relationship develops. My loves. My passions. My best jokes. My classic stories. My dreams. Maybe even, if I'm brave enough, my fears and vulnerabilities.

Our learners are no different. There are certainly going to be things we learn about them in a hurry, based on few interactions, but letting these relationships grow and flourish throughout our time together, whether it be a term or an entire year, is essential. Being mindful and respectful of the backgrounds, cultures, and beliefs of our students helps us ensure that we're providing a learning environment where they can grow, regardless of the age and stage we get 'em at. As they give us the gift of their story, it's up to us to choose what we do with it.

You know what I certainly don't want to talk about when I meet someone with whom I'm trying to build a relationship? The things I suck at. My inadequacies and deficiencies. The things I don't like about me. If someone comes in hot, telling me what I'm not good at and how they're going to fix it all and make me better, I'm immediately out (and cursing like a mother at them in my head).

Instead, new relationships inspire me to show what I bring to the table. Focusing on strengths and passions is where the relationship-building magic happens. Finding ways for students to express their love and passions is how I show them I see them, value them, and care about them.

Thinking about the things we do know about our students can be quite the trip. Consider just a couple of them (past or present) and see what you can come up with. Not the bullshit superficial stuff like their perceived motivators and triggers or locker numbers. I'm talking about the stuff that makes them who they are.

My Name Is ___ and I Like ___

Making a list of likes and dislikes in September is a favorite icebreaker. I've done polls on favorite songs and made playlists to blast as kids enter the room. I've learned about the latest TikTok sensation, the YouTube rockstars, weed pens—our job is to know the things that make our students feel seen. To know a kid's pronouns and favorite food, color, or TV show is great, but it's what you do with that information that matters. I've used it in all sorts of ways, like sticking that list of likes on a bulletin board to use as conversation starters. Those conversations can lead you to places that take your breath away, and phrases like "Tell me more" or "Why do you think" set the stage for them to continue.

Rockstar bus driver Marlena had been warned to be ready for a troublemaker who would be on her route—so she was ready for him on day one.

Marlena's Story

He turned out to be the most hilarious kid I'd ever driven. He was blunt and unfiltered. He loved video games and asked what games I liked to play. He told me all about his favorites and the YouTube videos he was creating. I knew this kid had my heart when I found myself watching gamers on YouTube so we'd have something to chat about. I loved every minute of it. He unknowingly reminded me of my why and gave me a reason to look forward to my drive. In return, I gave him the best year I could on that bus.

The way Marlena gathered information about what this kid loved and was passionate about it is an incredible testament to the power of knowing and using those likes to build connections.

One of my other favorite strategies that allows me to learn a lot about students is the Dreams, Needs, and Abilities (DNA) inventory introduced to me by educator Tom Hierck. He suggests that "the more teachers can tap into what motivates students and what students bring to the classroom each day, the more they can target instruction to those needs."[9] Since students' DNA impacts their experience in the classroom, incorporate it into your lessons and relationships.

Dreams: What do you wonder about? What do you hope to learn this year? Where do you want to go in life?

Needs: How can I help you? How can I be a better teacher for you? What frustrates you?

Abilities: What are you AMAZING at? What are you an expert in? What is something you can teach me?

Using this information to plan targeted, whole-group instruction can be fascinating. Dream about speaking Spanish in Spain? Let's learn some! Love drawing rainbows? Teach us! Need help with scissor skills?

Let's practice! Have no idea where to start with social justice to make a difference? Let's figure it out together!

Connecting with Caregivers

I often ask parents, caregivers, and even classroom friends, "What do you love about [name]?" This question can prompt some interesting answers. I've watched best friends giggle as they try to put into words what they love about their friend. Parents have looked at their child with tears in their eyes and said, "I don't think I've ever told you this, but what I love most about you is . . ." Some have a moment with their child they may never have had otherwise. A few years back, I asked this question of a father of one of our learners. He smiled, bowed his head, looked up with a tear in his eye, and said, "Please remember, he is my sunshine." You best believe I remembered that moment all year long.

See, these babes, regardless of age, are not ours. They belong to their families. Someone in the world of most every student has an answer to the question of what they love about them. Knowing that helps me focus on my incredible gratitude that I have this time with someone who is so loved.

Own a Fart

Since my very first year of teaching, I have taken responsibility for embarrassing farts. Listen, I would much prefer that farts were seen as natural, but I can't control social norms. Whenever I tell someone this, I inevitably get a "Why the heck would you do that?" which brings me to a story about my grade three teacher.

It was close to dismissal time. We were standing at our desks, and I peed my pants. Not like a little dribble, a floor- and tights-soaking pee. My teacher noticed before anyone else and came over, relaxed but urgent, and immediately "spilled" water on the floor from her coffee cup. She apologized for being so clumsy and asked me to go get the caretaker so we could mop it up. I relive that moment over and over again, so, when I finally moved into a classroom of my own, I vowed that I would "spill water" any chance I got to protect a student's dignity.

Little did I know just how many farts I would take responsibility for over the years. When someone lets out an audible toot, I immediately say, "I'm so sorry. Excuse me!" to take unwanted attention away from the gassy culprit. Sometimes it works. Sometimes it doesn't. But watching a child shrug their shoulders and point at me as their cheeks glow red with embarrassment brings me joy.

Need proof? I had a student in my very first classroom who was new to Canada, and on his very first day, he accidentally passed gas on a rumbly, plastic chair. He graduated recently and sent me a card thanking me for the impact I had on his educational career and listed some things he learned from me. Number one on the list? "Surround yourself with people who care about you so much they'd be willing to take ownership of a fart that is actually yours," signed, "Forever grateful."

"Own a fart" is essentially code for "maintain their dignity." Whether it's doing something or not doing something to preserve a learner's dignity in the classroom, it will undoubtedly strengthen the relationship.

Student Resume

I've always found the end of my time with a class to be a roller coaster of emotions. For the most part, we're usually ready to move on from one another. Not in an "I can't wait to get rid of you" way, but more in the spirit of "Our work here is done." Such an ending is an exciting time to reflect on how far we've come together and what the future may hold.

When you have to pass your students on to the next teacher, write the good stuff first. As you transition them into the next phase, consider making a little one-page (hell, even half-page) resume, showcasing their strengths and passions instead of highlighting their needs and troubles. Share what you love about them and learned from them. What do they bring to a classroom community to build it up? Talk those kids up. Share the love. Get the next teacher feeling grateful that they get to spend time with these superstars.

Susan is going to bring this chapter home, as her story embodies the holy work we do. We all have biases about our own "that one kid." The extraordinary part is when they prove us wrong.

Susan's Story

I had "that" class. I was in the final stages of my MEd, which I was sure was going to be my exit strategy from the classroom, when I found myself unexpectedly pregnant with our third child. I was teaching a 3/4 multigrade classroom and had a few regular lid-flippers. Then there was Jaxon. He was "that kid." The school system didn't fit Jaxon, and he'd given up trying to fit in.

I used every tool I had to make school work for this kid, but I couldn't get him to buy into it. I can't remember the date, but I do remember the moment perfectly. The kids were heading to French, and Jaxon refused to leave my room. He sat on the floor behind my desk, knees tucked up, head buried. I knew that nothing in my instructional toolkit was going to work. I needed to start pulling from my connection toolkit instead. So, I sat on the floor with him. We didn't talk, we just sat, until he looked up at me and asked, "Well, aren't you mad?"

Seeing the tears in his eyes, I knew that, in this moment of vulner-ability, he was letting me in. The next morning, he brought me a drawing he had sketched the night before. He left it on my desk and didn't say a word. I caught him at recess and asked him to tell me about it. Never had I heard him speak so much or be so lit up about anything. I realized this kid didn't need academics; he needed connection so the world could see him light up like that every day.

> I made it my mission to learn everything I could about Jaxon: he loved to draw and play Minecraft, and his cat Loki was his best friend. I loved that boy so much it hurt. While there were still hard days, they grew further apart. When I would come to school so ill with morning sickness, Jaxon would notice the peppermints I was eating, and, magically, mint gum would show up on my desk. The year ended, and I promised Jaxon I would send him pictures of my baby when she arrived in August.
>
> My daughter was born August 16, 2017. On August 19, Jaxon and his family were in a car accident. His father and older brother passed in the accident. Jaxon died on August 20, donating his organs to save five other children.
>
> In the moment when my grief for Jaxon was at its peak and in the millions of moments afterward, I knew that if I could love "that" kid so ferociously, then I was exactly where I needed to be: in the classroom with "those" kids. Losing Jaxon forever shifted my perspective of my purpose as an educator. Truthfully, if "those" kids leave my room every day feeling loved beyond measure, then my life's purpose has been met.

We owe it to every single one of our students to reflect on the hard questions. To celebrate their strengths. To give second and hundredth and millionth chances. To examine our own stories and our biases and make a change for every Jaxon out there. Susan didn't expect Jaxon to adapt to her. Instead, she adapted to him. I think it is safe to say she doesn't regret it one damn bit.

Wrapping Up and Moving On

Our biases will, without a doubt, have an impact on and sometimes cloud the way we come to understand another's story, but how you see the kids you serve and the people around you—in the staff room, halls, bus, and playground—can be exactly where things shift. It is the assessment—the gathering of data to make up the story—that can create remarkable room for insights and growth. We hope this chapter provides a map for your questions about why kids (and other people) do the things they do. Not to excuse, condone, or permit, but to allow for some space to make sense of it all so that you can continue to be clear on the difference you are making. Here are a few final notes from our now-familiar three, two, one.

Three things to try

- Make a list of the top three things your students this year are jacked about.
- What do you know—really know—about the first three students who come to mind?
- Get a fart machine and/or be prepared to take the fall for the farters, when necessary.

Two quotes to consider

"The human soul does not want to be advised or fixed or saved, it simply wants to be witnessed . . . exactly as it is." —Parker Palmer

"Don't judge a book by its cover." —George Eliot

One question to answer

- Think of that one student who proved you wrong—one who pleasantly surprised you when your expectations were minimal. What amazed you most about their story?

4

Trauma in the Classroom

One of the most important discussions in education these days revolves around the idea of teachers becoming trauma-informed. But what does it mean to be trauma-informed? And why is it so damn important? I appreciate that I might come in a little heavy on this belief, but without a doubt in my mind, emotional wellness is the foundation of any healthy school division. This might be the most critical information in this book, so a little warning: prepare your hearts. This chapter is long. And heavy. So, get some snacks and take deep breaths as you sink in with us. We've got you.

We considered splitting this chapter in two, but we have separated trauma and racism for far too long. If you want to become trauma-informed, addressing systemic oppression and racism absolutely must be a part of it. To understand racism, you must understand trauma. Trauma is embedded into every culture on this planet.[1] Because of this, we weave the consequences of systemic oppression throughout our discussion of trauma. Further, we have to understand how our own trauma histories show up in the classroom. Let's start with what trauma is, exactly.

What Is Trauma?

Many have attempted to define trauma via checklists, but having an experience(s) that can mess up the way you function in this world is so much more common than we care to admit. The definition of trauma that makes the most sense to me is simply this: trauma is any experience encoded in terror.[2] Why do some kids seem so much more resilient than others? Why do some teachers thrive with the toughest kids? What I've come to understand through that definition of trauma is that it's not necessarily an experience that causes it, it's how any experience is encoded and processed that determines the body's response.

I am not a trauma researcher, but what I want to highlight is the importance and undeniable impact of traumatic experiences on learning and, even more important, how trauma can have a significant impact on teachers.[3]

Adverse Childhood Experiences

In their groundbreaking study, Felitti and colleagues identified ten childhood experiences that may predict significant struggles in adulthood.[4] The Adverse Childhood Experiences (ACEs) Scale includes three broad categories: abuse, neglect, and household dysfunction. The assessment is simple: a "yes" answer to any of these ten items counts as a point, and the more points scored, the higher the risk.

Did a parent or other adult in the household often or very often . . .
1. Swear at you, insult you, put you down, or humiliate you or act in a way that made you afraid that you might be physically hurt?
2. Push, grab, slap, or throw something at you or ever hit you so hard that you had marks or were injured?
3. Did an adult or person at least five years older than you ever touch or fondle you or have you touch their body in a sexual way or attempt or actually have oral, anal, or vaginal intercourse with you?

Did you feel often or very often that . . .

4. No one in your family loved you or thought you were important or special or your family didn't look out for each other, feel close to each other, or support each other?

5. You didn't have enough to eat, had to wear dirty clothes, and had no one to protect you or your parents were too drunk or high to take care of you or take you to the doctor if you needed it?

6. Were your parents ever separated or divorced?

7. Was your mother or stepmother pushed, grabbed, slapped, or had something thrown at her?

8. Did you live with anyone who was a problem drinker or alcoholic or who used street drugs?

9. Was a household member depressed or mentally ill, or did a household member attempt suicide?

10. Did a household member go to prison?

As you review these questions, you will likely ask (as many do) why certain other experiences didn't make the list (e.g., the death of a sibling or surviving a car accident). It's not that these things aren't relevant; it's just that in the study's large sample, certain experiences showed more predictive power than others.

Anyone can calculate their ACEs score, and the body of research is readily available. Many researchers have suggested that having just any four items appears to be, without intervention or corrective experiences, the number that will result in difficulty functioning in adulthood, including an increase in addiction, interactions with the law, and suicidal ideation and completion. Just four.

In *Kids These Days*, I focused a lot on the ACEs research, and I still refer to it and use it in training school-based mental health professionals. But since then, I have learned so much about just how complex trauma and our responses to it are for everyone. A single score is a starting point; the context of how someone has responded to those experiences is equally, if not far more, important. We want to convey that the complexities that can show up in the classroom are far more representative than any single metric. We also have to be conscious of the lack of diversity in much of the research we often refer to as gospel when understanding people who have been traumatized.

The Complexities of Trauma

Researchers have recently offered valuable input into the neuroscience of trauma, providing insight into how the brain operates and how trauma can affect learning (and teaching). At its heart is the understanding of emotional dysregulation. However, the vast majority of clinical research is seldom used in direct patient care.[5,6] Furthermore, culture, race, and gender are very poorly represented when it comes to trauma research. It's imperative that we take a moment to shed some light on this. Please know that the sections that follow are not just specific to trauma, but I hope will serve as a starting point to increase our understanding that most (if not all) challenging behaviors you experience as a teacher within the classroom have a story behind them.

The Relationship between White Privilege and Trauma

I think it's so important to stay in my own lane (although I'll admit I often cut people off and get escorted back to my lane on a daily basis). We knew in this book we needed to talk about race and racism. There are many people who know better about this than we do (see Jesse Thistle and Jesse Lipscombe, for two). So, when we considered (and reconsidered) this chapter on trauma, talking about racism and anti-racism scared us. It's so much easier to talk about the facts: How to assess trauma. How it shows up. The steps to treat it. In this unknown-to-us, emotion-filled territory of racism, what if we fuck it up, say something wrong or offensive? But here's what I do know about: white privilege and what it's like to be a racist. And how even when we don't want to consider how it might be embedded in our relationships, our culture, our classrooms, it is. Not talking about it is no longer an option.

White privilege can be defined as the societal privilege that benefits white people over non-white people.[7] The unearned advantages afforded to people who are—or are assumed to be, based on complexion and related physical features—of European ancestry. The notion of white privilege derives from critical race theory (CRT), a branch of jurisprudence that argues race-based preferences and biases are embedded in established law and policy and are not simply a function of preferential or biased interpretation and enforcement of these rules.[8] I have never had to talk to my children about safety when they are at the mall or out for a walk because of the color of their skin. That is white privilege.

These biases are rooted in European colonialism and the Atlantic slave trade.[9,10] How, you ask, was it ever decided, that white-skinned people were the "better" ones? Well, that takes us to white supremacy.

White supremacy is the belief that white people are superior to those of other races and thus should dominate them.[11] Its purpose is the maintenance and defense of a system of wealth, power, and privilege. White supremacy has roots in the now-discredited doctrine of scientific racism,[12] where data were used to suggest that white people were better, smarter, and purer, thus acting as a key justification for colonialism.[13] White supremacy has flourished over many generations, and we have barely begun to address the harm that is so embedded in every institution in North America. In contemporary usage, "white supremacist" has been used to describe some groups espousing ultra-nationalist, racist, or fascist doctrines, but white supremacy is much more pervasive and mainstream than that.

I grew up in rural Alberta, Canada, and I don't remember seeing a person of color until the first Black kid came to our school in 1984. I remember feeling that Black and Indigenous people were to be feared. Driving through Indigenous reservations meant going fast because I'd been told "it's not safe." I would often make fun of the names in the phone book or speak with accents in a derogatory way, which was, unfortunately, always good for a laugh. It took a very long time for me to see the impact of these actions.

With respect to our Indigenous history in Canada, I again confess that I have been remarkably unaware, and not because there aren't resources available. In my experience, however, we've only just begun to talk as a society about the profound impact the Indian residential school system (IRS)[14] has had on our kids, teachers, classrooms, and families.

Two primary objectives of the IRS were to remove and isolate children from the influence and cultures of their families of origin and to assimilate them into the dominant culture. These objectives were based on the assumption that Indigenous cultures and spiritual beliefs were inferior. Canada's IRS system is not a historical experience. The last operating IRS closed in 1996.[15] Children who were apprehended from their homes, forced away from their families, and many times abused and neglected are now in their thirties, forties, and fifties.[16] Although the IRS eventually shut down, all of those children (and the children before them) were cast back into the world without corrective experiences. Despite many Indigenous peoples having spoken of the frequent death and murder of children in the IRS system, the initial discovery of the bodies of 215 children in graves at the Kamloops IRS, located on the Tk'emlúps te Secwépemc First Nation, in May 2021 has just begun to draw light upon the many atrocities that occurred.[17] And the practice of apprehending children extended well beyond the IRS system, intensifying from 1950 to 1980, during a period called the Sixties Scoop.[18]

Trauma can happen in many contexts. Philosopher Kate Manne points out that white women, in particular, in an effort to "lean in" in leadership roles, sometimes "lean down" on women of color in an effort to work against misogynistic ideals.[19] This makes a serious cause for reflection on how we show up with our colleagues, not just for the students we serve, and it's critical we acknowledge this practice exists and have open, honest discussions about it with our teams.

Kids in Care

When it comes to kids I've worked with, I suppose I thought I'd addressed some of my biases. I had empathy for, recognized the importance of advocating for, and felt compelled to work for organizations that served kids in care.[20,21] They have a huge place in my heart. I want to protect and advocate for them. But, turns out, that doesn't mean I didn't have biases about them or how they got to where they were.

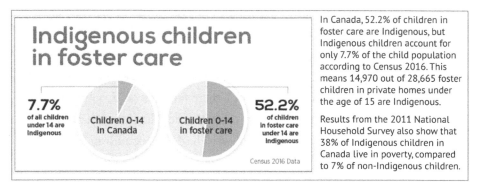

In Canada, 52.2% of children in foster care are Indigenous, but Indigenous children account for only 7.7% of the child population according to Census 2016. This means 14,970 out of 28,665 foster children in private homes under the age of 15 are Indigenous.

Results from the 2011 National Household Survey also show that 38% of Indigenous children in Canada live in poverty, compared to 7% of non-Indigenous children.

First Nations Child and Family Services (2020).
Reducing the number of Indigenous children in care.

Here's why it's important for us to talk about this, particularly in this chapter on trauma. When you are part of a group that has survived generations of abuse, neglect, and trauma, you will struggle and you will be treated differently in this world. Intergenerational trauma is an established psychological concept that means that the skills (or lack thereof) one generation learned for coping in life will be passed on to the next generation. You can't give away something you've never received. Intergenerational trauma has been well documented in many instances, including among Holocaust survivors,[22] refugee families,[23] and Indigenous communities.

The ramifications of the cultural genocide that was the IRS and the subsequent intergenerational trauma that persists today are reflected in our schools in so many ways. Many children in the foster care system are Indigenous; in fact, in the province where I sit, Indigenous children (ages 0–17 years) account for about 10 percent of the population but represent 70 percent of children and youth in care.[24]

Further, the suicide rates for Indigenous youth are six times higher than for non-Indigenous children.[25] They are also diagnosed with ADHD at a rate six times higher than non-Indigenous children; this is likely less reflective of legitimate ADHD presentations than of emotional dysregulation from generations of abuse, neglect, and trauma.[26]

Finally, you might be shocked to discover that 48 percent of Indigenous youth do not achieve a high school diploma,[27] and in Nunavut, 73 percent of the Indigenous population has less than a high school education and only 15 percent has a post-secondary education.[28] The ramifications of these numbers can be incredibly impactful as this generation sets out to raise the next generation.

Maintaining the Momentum of Movements

Now, I'll be painfully honest with you. I am a psychologist who spews the importance of connection. So, I didn't want to be divisive in jumping on a Black (or Indigenous or Trans) Lives Matter bandwagon. We're wired for connection after all, aren't we? Don't all lives matter? Ugh.

Then I started to listen and finally understand. Of course, all lives matter. But we have to acknowledge that certain lives haven't mattered for centuries and, largely, still don't. Because of that, they've paid a price. It looks like trauma. And addiction. And rage. And it's justified.

You can't judge people at the finish line until you've assessed where they started. I had a lot of things in my favor when I started this human race: I'm white, straight, able-bodied, educated, middle- to upper-class. In North America in particular, people who fall outside of the white, heterosexual, middle-to-upper class, able-bodied norms often have less power and experience marginalization in the form of under-education, poverty, and unemployment.[29] If you look at someone who stands on a stage, speaks, writes, creates, teaches, but did not start in a place of privilege, imagine how much harder, faster, stronger they've had to work than I have to get to a similar place in life.

Does that mean white, straight, educated, able-bodied people don't struggle? No. It means that if they did struggle, it wasn't because of their skin color or sexuality. Does it mean that some Black, Indigenous, trans, or disabled people have had it "easier" than some white people? Well, I promise you it would be extremely difficult to find data to support that. Further, we're not talking about a single experience; we should be most concerned about what it looks like for the whole of a particular community.

Ijeoma Oluo, the author of *So You Want to Talk about Race* said, "The beauty of anti-racism is that you don't have to pretend to be free of racism to be an anti-racist. Anti-racism is the commitment to fight racism wherever you find it, including in yourself. And it's the only way forward."[30] And forward we will proceed.

Marginalization and Systemic Oppression

So, where does this leave us? We now understand that oppression, at its core, means that some people have more social power and access to privilege than others, which oftentimes leads to oppression of less-powerful groups. Systemic oppression is present when the laws, policies, and practices of governments or institutions favor the powerful over other, typically marginalized groups. Oppression comes in many forms, with racism and sexism being two of the more frequently used examples. People can experience different kinds of oppression at the same time. In fact, when there is an intersection of multiple experiences of oppression, the results are increasingly more devastating.[31] For example, if you are a Black, transgender, working-class student, each of those marginalizing factors compounds, making it that much more difficult to show up in the world.

I've been tremendously fortunate to be guided through my blundering growth in this area by patient, generous activists, educators, persons of color, and Indigenous Elders. At home, we use LaNesha Tabb and Naomi O'Brien's *A White Families' Guide to Talking about Racism*[32] as a roadmap for discussing racism with our kids. Prompted by the guide, they asked us: "Mom, Daddy, have you ever done something racist?" We both explained that we absolutely had. All three of our babes looked disgusted and mortified. "What did you do?" they asked. I told them about when I used to mock accents and names and that I'd made assumptions based on skin color. Aaron told them he often used to say that certain people should just work harder instead of "waiting for handouts," not understanding what so many of the people around us had endured or survived. Later, I had similar conversations with my parents and with our mostly white team. Hard conversations are never easy (you're welcome for that brilliant insight), but they are absolutely necessary. Just like with emotional regulation, you can't tell people how to do it, you have to show them.

Do the Next Right Thing

From this psychologist's chair, I have to tell you that it's often not what happens in individual therapy sessions that has the most profound impact on healing, but what happens in day-to-day interactions. We have failed, I think, to equip the adults who are most accessible to children on a daily basis with even the basics for understanding difficult emotional experiences. Many times, I have sat with teachers who, when we talk about trauma, say: "But I'm not a social worker. I'm not trained to handle these things. I got into teaching to teach. Not provide therapy." My response to that, in my head (and sometimes out loud), is "bullshit." If I take you back to why you got into this business, I'll bet you'll tell me it's because someone inspired you. They got it. They saw you. Or they didn't get it and you didn't want that to happen to other children. You got into this because, at your core, you understand the importance of human connection.

The goal isn't necessarily to equip you with the skills to "fix" trauma. That, sweet teachers, is not your job. In fact, there are no fixes. Even if you're all sorts of amazing (which you probably are), you cannot single-handedly alter multiple generations of abuse, neglect, or trauma. You can't protect our most vulnerable children from all the racism and discrimination they face every day. What's so critically important to know is that empathy is created when we understand the meaning behind behavior. I can promise you that understanding and developing empathy for your most emotionally dysregulated students (and colleagues) will enlighten you with an understanding of how trauma can affect the ways we show up in the world. Then it will more clearly guide our responses and our teaching.

Representation Matters

When talking about marginalization, we have to talk about representation. Representation matters. Of course, it does! If you're surrounded by people who don't look like you or sound like you, how many more barriers does that present when attempting to trust them? In Canada, most teachers are white and heterosexual.[33],[34] If you're in a position of privilege, building communities and resources where kids can see themselves in books, lessons, and faces in the crowd helps those brains regulate faster and learn better.[35] And, turns out, those brains teach better, too.

So many of you have talked about how difficult it is to teach in school systems where racism and marginalization are alive and well within the staff population. Sweet lord. You've said: "We have been saying this for years and no one was listening. As the only Black/Indigenous/gay/trans/fill-in-the-blank teacher in my school, there have been significant challenges at times to be seen, heard, and understood

at staff meetings, on committees, or when I speak up for students."
This, if I can be so bold, is a much bigger concern even than how the
children are treated, simply because if those of us holding our students
aren't OK, these babes don't stand a chance. They're watching how we
treat each other. Remember: you can't tell a kid how to be antiracist or
inclusive; you have to show them.

Our Own Trauma Histories

I want to talk about what an ACEs score means for you. Many of us
who serve others in our work, particularly children, come with our
own trauma histories. In fact, we all do. We all have a story of loss or
pain, to some degree. I can't tell you how many times teachers have
told me after a talk, "My ACEs score is eight" or "I have them all." Many
of us function well and serve others beautifully, not in spite of our own
trauma histories, but because of them.

Your history, and especially an ACEs score, doesn't define you.
Equally important in the processes of learning a history and holding
space for the hard stuff is understanding and acknowledging all the
corrective experiences that helped buffer it. What, or who, has helped
make you great? How, on your best days, are you able to do this incredible work?

There's very little discussion around what happens when teachers
experience trauma as a result of teaching. How do we address it when
we've been part of a violent episode with a child or had to intervene
in a school shooting? The answer isn't an obvious four-step response,
but I promise you, just as with the babes you teach, naming it to tame
it will be key. Seeking support as soon as you're able after a traumatic
experience can be extremely helpful in the healing process. Sometimes,
just slowing down long enough to reflect will help. How does your own
parents' divorce, your own experience with abuse, or your own story
around loss and grief impact the babes you're walking home? It's not

that you even have to alter the way you show up, but you can't address what you don't acknowledge.

My ACEs score is 3. Laurie's is 4. As Dr. Brené Brown said: "What if we were willing to acknowledge our own hurt and pain and in doing so make sure to not diminish the hurt and pain of others? We could change the world."[36] Amen.

The Trouble with Trauma-Informed Schools

There's been a wide-sweeping initiative to address this evil force called trauma in education. It's necessary and overdue. As a number of recent researchers have brought to light, however, without proper guidance or a systematic approach, good intentions often exacerbate the problem. The essential components of a trauma-informed approach have not been clearly operationalized, especially for school settings. These approaches appear under different terms, like "trauma-informed care," "trauma-sensitive," and "trauma-informed system."[37,38] To date, there is no consensus on the use of these terms, which makes efforts to both implement and study trauma-informed approaches challenging. One of the biggest mistakes is implementing these approaches without first understanding the context of the behavior that any one child presents with. For example, although initiatives like mindfulness programs are helpful, it can be difficult, if not harmful, to expect a student who is currently experiencing an abusive situation at home to sit quietly with their thoughts. Further, disciplining them if they're unable to be mindful can be devastating. The intention is beautiful. The outcome is not.

If disciplinary practices do not follow suit (e.g., your district is still widely employing out-of-school suspensions with little or no effort focused on re-entry plans or how to stay connected to the student during the suspension), the result is even more disconnection among staff, students, and parents. (See chapter 7 for more about disciplinary responses.) Understanding individual students' stories from a trauma-informed and relationship-focused perspective is how we develop the most successful trauma-informed schools. I have developed a training specific for mental health professionals in K-12 education, as there is very little standard of practice for those doing mental health work in schools.[39]

Trauma Affects Teaching

Trauma is an issue of equity. Students who experience trauma on its own will have their educational attainment impacted, and it will disproportionately affect students of color, Indigenous students, students with disabilities, those living in poverty, 2SLGBTQ+ students, and others who experience marginalization.[40,41] "Without intervention, trauma can have a significant impact on life outcomes for students. Even one adverse childhood experience has been shown to decrease postsecondary educational achievement by 20 percent."[42] Further, it's safe to assume that educators who feel unsupported and unseen will struggle to serve students who need it most. We know that almost three in every four teachers report mental health–related concerns as a direct result of feeling unsupported in this profession, particularly in our new pandemic-infused world.[43] We need to do better.

Most often, our most significant traumas happen in the context of relationships. Just look at the ACEs criteria: every single one of the "big ones" has something to do with an interaction with another human being. But it's also in relationships where healing occurs. The trickiest part is convincing those babes you serve who have experienced trauma at the hands of an adult that you, as an adult, are safe. Sometimes this can't be done in a few interactions or even a school year. Our job is simply to do the best we can with what we've got from a place of empathy. It is in the benevolent experiences where the healing lives. Let me tell you more.

More Than an ACEs Score

The World Health Organization advises: "Health is more than the absence of disease."[44] What do we do when kids experience significantly high ACEs scores or other experiences encoded in terror? It's only recently that researchers have begun talking about the importance of positive or corrective experiences as mitigators to ACEs.[45] Many have highlighted the critical importance of the joint assessment of the corrective experiences and ACEs as an approach to better target needs and interventions and promote well-being.[46,47]

One of my favorite assessments is called the Benevolent Childhood Experiences (BCEs) Scale.[48] It's brief and culturally sensitive, and the early research suggests it's robust and reliable. It measures aspects of internal perceived safety (e.g., Did you have beliefs that gave you comfort?), external perceived safety (e.g., Did you have at least one caregiver with whom you felt safe?), security and support (e.g., Was there an adult who could provide you with support or advice?), and positive and predictable qualities of life (e.g., Did you have a predictable home routine, like regular meals and a regular bedtime?).

Similar to the ACEs Scale, this is a ten-point scale that requires an assessment of the child (or yourself) regarding the corrective experiences you may have received. If you experienced any of the listed items before the age of eighteen, you get a point. In this instance, the more points the better.

During your first 18 years of life, did you:
1. Have at least one caregiver with whom you felt safe?
2. Have at least one good friend?
3. Have beliefs that gave you comfort?
4. Like school?
5. Have at least one teacher who cared about you?
6. Have good neighbors?
7. Have an adult (not a parent/caregiver or the person from #1) who could provide you with support or advice?

8. Have opportunities to have a good time?
9. Like yourself or feel comfortable with yourself?
10. Have a predictable home routine, like regular meals and a regular bedtime?

What I want to highlight here is the significant influence that teachers have in mitigating trauma. You will notice that at least half of these items directly involve those of you in the education system. Never underestimate the power of having "at least one teacher who cared."

Consider Yourself Trauma-Informed When . . .

In reviewing the research and taking into account what we know from both theory and practice, at minimum, these things need to be present to be trauma-informed:

1. You understand that, although there are certain experiences that will most likely result in trauma, the definition of a traumatic experience is "anything encoded in terror." This means that an awareness of another's story is much more informative than a score or an account of behavior.

2. You know individuals cannot heal alone from trauma; fostering a connected relationship is key to healing. Further, many of the most significant traumas occur as a result of a rupture in a relationship. As psychiatrist Bessel van der Kolk so eloquently states, "Being able to feel safe with other people is probably the single most important aspect of mental health; safe connections are fundamental to meaningful and satisfying lives."[49]

3. You know that an awareness of your own story or trauma history is critical to how you will walk others through theirs.

4. You believe that traumatic stories can be repaired and that this will always involve creating a safe place to make sense of the experience first. Then, and only then, will behavioral shifts follow.

5. You know that remaining trauma-informed will require a continued commitment to understanding the advances in this field and how trauma is inextricably connected to racism, and you will continue to engage in learning from reliable, empirically supported research.

If these five statements make sense to you and align with the culture of your school, then being trauma-informed is fundamentally important to the people you work with. This is not only necessary, it's critical as we step into the next chapter in education.

A Word on Disclosures

Educators may sometimes receive disclosures of abuse or neglect. In those moments, there are three basic, but so very important, phrases that can help support a student when responding to their disclosures:

1. "Thank you for telling me."
2. "I'm sorry this happened."
3. "I will take it from here." or "How can I help?" (This depends on the situation and the policies of your respective district.)

Typically, an abuse disclosure from a minor requires a call to police and/or protective services. It's their job to investigate. Having worked with at-risk babes for most of my career, I can tell you that the moments of disclosure can be some of the scariest. You might not want to be the one to call. It might be difficult to trust the system to support the child and the family in ways that will be most helpful. Consulting with colleagues and being clear on the expectations around disclosures before you ever receive one can help prepare you for when (not if) you do. Know that these moments are often important times of transition toward healing.

Laurie will now share the things we want you to consider as you step into any classroom, so you can remember that every student has a story. And so do you.

We All Have a Story

Trauma. It's a word I didn't hear during my university education. No one mentioned the fact that everyone has a story and that trauma affects all we do.

The night before I began my education degree, I had an experience I "encoded in terror." They had been frequent in the decade that led up to this night. On the eve of my university orientation, a relationship I'd been involved in since I was fourteen ended. It was terrifying and freeing at the same time. That night, I flushed a wedding ring down the toilet and vowed on the floor of a hotel bathroom that nothing would stop me from getting this degree. It was my dream. And no one was taking it from me.

I got an hour's sleep, woke up, and headed off to my orientation. Some poor first-year student had the unfortunate luck of being paired with me on the tour. As we walked along, she asked, "So, um, where are you from? Are you in a relationship? Where are you living?"

I laughed. Much harder than I needed to. She looked concerned. I responded with, "You're not going to believe this . . ." She looked even more concerned. It all came spilling out. The events of the previous night, the history, the gaslighting, the innocence that was taken from me, all of it. It was way too many details for a stranger, but at this point I was all in. After a long silence, I took a deep breath and said, "Thanks. I needed to let that out." She smiled nervously and said words I'll never forget: "You seemed so 'normal' when we met. I never would've guessed all that happened to you literally eleven hours ago. . . . I'm glad you're here."

Her words propelled me many times through the next two years. "I'm glad you're here." She didn't fix it for me. She couldn't. No one could. But her words and all the souls who watched me find myself over those years are the reason I actually completed the degree. As a result, I have an immense sense of gratitude for this title of teacher.

I'm not someone you might typically associate with trauma when you see me, a white, educated woman who is now married with three kids. I'm not embarrassed about the trauma I've endured. However, it's a story I share if and when I'm comfortable. Comparing one experience to another is futile; yet, an awareness that the stories we hold impact how we show up is fundamental to staying healthy in this business.

If only our learners would come to us with their hands up saying, "Oooh! Trauma? Let me tell you all about it!" it would make this hard space of teaching so much easier. However, it is rare for someone to feel comfortable sharing their story before a relationship has been built. Which is just fine because guess what, sweet teacher friend? You don't need the details surrounding someone's history and trauma to be able to provide safety, understanding, and empathy. The specifics of someone's story aren't what matters. What matters is that they felt enough trust to come to you. What matters is that we're able to continually humble ourselves to see beyond the behavior and to offer time and grace in order to meet our kids right where they are with whatever story they come with. It doesn't matter if you believe another's trauma is "bad" enough or not. What matters is what we do with the information and the stories we are honored to hold. If it matters to them, it matters. If and when they do decide to share their story, what you do with it can either make or break the relationship. Choose wisely.

Some of My Teachers, So Far . . .

I cannot possibly comprehend all it means to experience trauma as a marginalized or oppressed person in our society. Trauma of marginalized people, trauma caused by systematic oppression, and trauma caused by the educational systems in which we teach are topics I'm only starting to learn about. I'm incredibly grateful for the knowledge and experiences of people like Joe Dombrowski, Shelley Moore, Alyssa Gray-Tyghter, Megan Tipler, Helen Vangool, Sarah Adomako-Ansah, Andrew Parker, and Vera Ahiyya. Taking this learning into our classroom is an important part of trying to address, learn from, and raise an understanding of the voices of those who have been silenced for so long.

One of the many lessons I've learned is the critical importance of doing my own research and reading about topics surrounding racism in education before seeking clarification from friends and mentors in the BIPOC community. Josh Parker says there is no single "trauma-informed or mindfulness strategy that is better than actually stopping the trauma to minoritized students brought on by racist practices."[50] The last thing the world needs is one more white person "helping" in a self-serving manner, the definition of white savior syndrome.

Brittany is a teacher whose words take me back to so many of my students. The story changes everything.

Brittany's Story

It wasn't until first recess when a mom showed up with a backpack that we realized something was very wrong. She broke down and told us that the day before her daughter had come home from school to find Mom's boyfriend passed out on the basement floor from an overdose, the needle still in his arm. Mom was overwhelmed and scared. I wondered just what my little grade three student had witnessed and held in her little heart over the past twenty-four hours. Of course, she forgot her backpack. What really stuck with me was that it seemed like a normal day. She'd shown no signs of trauma that morning when she arrived at school. The truth is, as teachers, we seldom know what happens when a student leaves our classroom.

We never truly know. This little one was likely not yet ready or able to verbalize what she had seen. And who knows? It could even be that the experience wasn't "encoded in terror." When we remind ourselves that there is likely a story in there somewhere, we get some grace in the process. It's often not because we're not teaching something right or they are resistant or "not ready to learn." There may just be so much more to the story, and remembering this might help us continue as our kids write the chapter of their books that we find ourselves a part of.

Brain, Not Behavior

In their book, *The Trauma-Informed School*, Jim Sporleder and Heather Forbes explain that if trauma is all a student knows, their brains are wired for fear.[51] "Their brains aren't 'bad' and their reactivity isn't necessarily 'wrong': it's a brain issue, not a behavioral issue." Understanding this, and that every learner comes with a story, is essential to recognizing the stress that trauma creates for those affected by it and to serving those in our care.

We cannot fix trauma. For a whole culture built upon "fixing" kids and "being the one" for every kid, this isn't an easy thing to hear. But I'll repeat: We're not in the business of fixing kids. To say that we are, implies that they are something to be fixed. That's just not true. This mindset can lead to savior syndrome,[52] which can have you believing you must "save" them all. Instead, I focus on the significant role of teachers in mitigating trauma.

There are a few tangible things to remember, including safety, predictability, acknowledgment, and joy, when you are most concerned about how a trauma history is showing up for you or your students. Let's unpack each of these here, as they relate specifically to trauma.

You Are Safe. Showing Them, Not Telling Them

For those who have experienced or are currently experiencing trauma, a feeling of safety is going to be of utmost importance. Is this a safe or scary place? Am I in the presence of someone who will keep me safe? Can I depend on this person, or do I need to manage this all on my own? Without feeling safe, our kids will not learn.

It's fair to say that every teacher wants to believe their classroom is perceived as a safe place by all students. But is it? Are there systems, practices, routines, or procedures that make every child safe? Critically examining and acknowledging our practices to ensure they are what's best for those we serve has to be where we start.

Even as I sit here typing, I realize there are things I'm doing that might not allow a child to feel as safe as they should. And, that's never OK. But challenges change us, so challenging myself and allowing others to challenge my procedures and practices will no doubt bring important and significant changes to ensure that all feel safe.

Some questions that might help in this process of providing a safe environment for all are the following:

- Am I enforcing rules or addressing needs?
- Is my tone of voice welcoming, or do I use it to punish?
- If what we permit, we promote, am I promoting that all are safe in our classroom environment?
- Are those who cannot "follow rules" guaranteed both physical and emotional safety?
- What strategies can I implement to ensure that all feel safe?
- Who can I learn more from?

A feeling of safety isn't going to be accomplished by a teacher telling a student they are safe. It's going to be accomplished with time, community, and connection.

I put an incredible amount of time into keeping things consistent and predictable for our learners. Visual schedules, consistent daily routines, and predictable common language are intentional strategies in developing a sense of safety. Proactive discussions on how it can feel when things don't go as planned and strategies to use when we face that disappointment are also helpful.

Back in my early days of teaching, I had a student who would lose it on special days, like pajama day or when we had assemblies. It always blew my mind. Why did he always have to react with anger and try to bolt when we were just trying to have some fun, dammit?!

Our incredible behavioral specialist came in on Hallo-fricking-ween to offer me some guidance. Let's just say, the day did not go well for him or for me. But he offered this revelation that still moves me:

"I know you see these as 'fun' days, but he doesn't. Your classroom provides him with consistency and predictability, which allows him to feel safe. But throwing in something novel? Something where he cannot use his 'successful' strategies to stay regulated? It's too much. He feels unsafe and that's why he runs. Reassure him. Affirm him to remind him he is safe. Bring him back to that feeling over and over again."

As we moved through the year with this little muffin, I learned so much about important research done by stress researcher Sonia Lupien[53] and her team at the Centre for Studies on Human Stress, which profoundly impacted my outlook and planning in our class-room. Their research has shown that for a situation to be stressful it must contain one or more of the following characteristics:

N - novelty; something new

U - unpredictability; no way of knowing it could occur

T - threat to the ego; feeling your competence is questioned

S - sense of control; feeling you have little or no control in a situation[54]

The more NUTS present, the higher your stress. On these special days, this sweet boy was overloaded with stress and felt like his safety was threatened. He handled it the only way he knew how, which was to flee. This lesson regularly reminds me that, for many, safety is directly related to consistency, predictability, and perceived control over any given situation. Grounding our kids with these elements is essential to their feeling of safety.

This isn't to say that everything can and will be controlled so that no student ever has to feel that their safety is threatened, but it does remind me that I need to put the time and effort into ensuring that we do the work to make our day-to-day interactions and activities as con-sistent as possible. It also assures me that having thoughtful discussions and building strategies to deal with perceived threats when they arise is critical to success.

Everyone Wants to Be Seen and Heard

I recognize you.

I see you.

I honor you.

I value you.

I accept you.

I am here.

You matter to me.

However you word it, acknowledging another human is powerful. It's what we all need. And it's the most important message we'll share in our classrooms.

As a teacher, especially a kindergarten teacher, I've always had the mindset that, as kids come into our community each year, it's up to me to adapt to them and not the opposite. It's not their job to adapt to the system. It's my job to adjust that system so they feel included and seen and to provide them with the time and opportunities to build their identity. It's not a matter of whether or not they are ready for me; it's a question of what I can do to prepare for them. Despite my own story, my own pain, the systems in place that lead to marginalization, the cries of "We've always done it this way," I can only serve all by first acknowledging them.

There are many ways this can be done. I bet you are doing all kinds of wonderful things right now that make the students you serve feel seen and valued. Here's the one we rarely consider: the power of just being with someone. That's it. Not fixing things or providing opinions and advice. It can be very hard and even painful to be with some kids. It can bring up our own trauma. It can bring out uncomfortable feelings. Being with can even make us feel ineffective because we're primed to be fixers. Being with is a critical choice we can all make, and it's a powerful tool when it comes to helping any human experiencing trauma.

So, what does this look like? It looks like proximity. Maybe even on the floor or under a table. It looks like sitting in the darkness until the light can seep back in. It looks like eye contact, a relaxed posture, a nod. It looks like you care. What does it sound like? It might sound like silence. Or a low hum. It might sound like, "I'm here for you if you need me," or "I don't know what to say right now, but I'm glad you told me," or "This sounds incredibly hard. Thank you for sharing."

Kevin, a bus driver, shared this story about a teenage girl who taught him about the power of holding space.

Kevin's Story

Every morning, I would greet Savannah with a smile and a friendly hello as she got on the bus. Some mornings she would respond, and others she would not, but I never gave her a hard time about it. I just smiled the same smile every morning. The front seat was hers, and I always felt like it was because she wanted to be close to me, but I didn't have a clue why.

I'm a talker. But Savannah? She wasn't. After months of driving her in silence, I heard Savannah's voice from the front seat one day. "Kevin? I need your help." She went into a story about how she didn't have a dad to guide her at home, but she needed to tell someone about some troubles at school. She didn't say, "I need advice." She said, "I need someone to know." I knew this was a time to listen and make sure she knew I cared. I would glance at her in my rearview mirror and just nod. As she shared, her face changed, and I knew I was making a difference.

I drove that girl for three more years. Some days were still silent, and some she would share the good and the bad. I never pushed her. I was just there if and when she did need me. On the last day

I drove her, she told me that without me listening, she worries she might have hurt herself because she never felt like people saw her. But because I did? She never carried through with her plans. I cried. She taught me so much about how not all kids need to hear me yammer away. Sometimes they just need me to listen and care.

Giving your energy to just being with someone sends a strong message that you care, that you see and value them. Observe. Hold space. Listen. Empower.

I've Got That Joy, Joy, Joy, Joy

We talk about joy a lot in this book. It is, after all, the most vulnerable emotion on the planet.[55] It is in this emotion where we are all at our best. Three things bring me the most joy in our classroom:

1. Being silly with the pure intention of getting our kids to laugh and actually getting that laugh;
2. Letting our kids or students take the lead; and
3. Ripping up plans (like actually, physically ripping them up) when things go to hell and refocusing on what our students need, which usually leads to the three Fs: food, fun, and fresh air. Telling a whole lecture hall, "Take a walk with me," can shake up any "lack of learning."

Bringing joy into our space can help lessen pain and connect us all. A good belly laugh, some silliness, a dance break—it doesn't take away the hard stuff, but it gives our bodies a physical reprieve that is so necessary to wellness. Bringing the joy is an incredible way to drop the cortisol and de-escalate the stress responses. We are all better for it, even if it's just momentarily.

It's incredibly important to me to mention that "finding the joy" is not meant to shame or guilt anyone who is unable to find it. My anxiety and depression mean that experiencing joy is sometimes literally impossible. Please know that is not what this is about. Joy can and will depend on mental health. If you struggle in this way, I see you. Be gentle with yourself on the days you simply cannot.

We shouldn't just be "doing school." We spend massive amounts of time in these spaces with these kids and colleagues. Who wants to be miserable? Resolve to bring joy into your classroom communities, hallways, and staff rooms to lessen stress and connect your community in the most wonderful way. It may sound scary, even exhausting. Just know that joy and learning go together.

A Trauma Story That Brings It All Home

In all your heartfelt stories about trauma, there was one I kept thinking about. It was from Kim, a teacher, and it addresses for me almost every part of this chapter and how it relates to our kids with trauma. See if you agree and if it stays with you like it did me.

Kim's Story

I once was privileged to know a beautiful blond-haired boy. I taught him in kindergarten when he was pudgy and cute and again in grade three, a taller, slimmer, quieter version of his kindergarten self. But I knew something was wrong. The light he'd had was gone. This beautiful soul was caught in the middle of trauma, not because he chose it, but because he lived it. This is not the story of a bad kid but about a terrible circumstance that brought me a great teaching joy moment.

Years later, I was called by the parole office to administer a placement test in reading and writing for an inmate heading to juvenile detention. I sat in a room waiting for the student, never imagining it would be him—that blond boy who had stolen my heart in kindergarten.

He was led into the room in shackles. I was in shock. I asked the guard to remove them. This student was no threat to me. The guard refused and said he was too dangerous. Too dangerous? What did this stupid guard know about this child and his situation? He didn't know the story of his life. When we completed the test, I let the guard know we were finished. I told my student that he did really well and I was so proud of him for keeping up with his learning under his current circumstances. That lovely boy said thank you and then told me a story.

He asked if I remembered a few years earlier when our school had been broken into and heavily damaged. I said I did, a little leery of what would come next. He asked if I remembered that the door to my room had been closed and my classroom left untouched. It was, in fact, the only door closed in the entire school when the RCMP and the teachers arrived in the morning. I was always curious why my room was the only one not destroyed in that break-in and I got my answer that day. He told me he was responsible for that. He told his crew that they could do anything they wanted to the school, but no one was to enter my room. He had shut the door. I didn't know what to say. I just hugged him and told him to take care of himself and that if he needed anything to come find me at the school.

I only saw that young man one more time, but it was not to hug him or talk to him or test him. I saw him the day his family buried him. And while the drummers played to send his soul up to the Creator, we danced our hearts out just for him.

Whether you know the details of the trauma or not, do not ever doubt that *you* have the power to make a difference in a child's life. *You* have the power to make them feel seen and heard. *You* have the power to show them that you will never stop believing in them (shackles or not). *You* can bring them joy.

Wrapping Up and Moving On

Trauma will show up in how you teach and how students learn, and the ramifications of multiple generations of systemic oppression will show up in our classrooms. It doesn't need to be a thing we fear or avoid, but, instead, it can be something we understand. That perspective shift will allow us to see more clearly the most important thing about trauma: the healing power of corrective experiences.

Three things to try

- Have students write a letter twice per year titled: "I wish my teacher knew . . ." Sometimes we make assumptions about what our students are thinking or experiencing. Give them a voice and see what they say.

- What brings joy to your staff room? Do one thing this week that might bring your colleagues joy. Donuts? Homemade muffins? A fart machine (clearly an important focus of this book)? The big people need a belly laugh. Trust us.

- Pass out a (small) treat at the beginning of a class and watch productivity explode. Now, sometimes forty mini packs of Skittles are not in the budget, but know that when you get anyone eating or drinking, their prefrontal cortex is on. Bringing them back to regulation will serve them (and you) so well.

Two quotes to consider

"Let's stop asking kids 'What's wrong with you?' and start asking 'What happened?' Then, let's be quiet and listen with compassion." —Jim Sporleder

"The single most important issue for traumatized people is to find a sense of safety in their own bodies." —Bessel van der Kolk

One question to answer

- In reviewing the five things we consider critical to becoming trauma-informed (see p. 91), how do you, your school, or your institution measure up?

Braving the Waves of Grief

This topic of grief and loss has taken up a lot of space in my mind and my heart. We're often scared to talk about it, as it's not something most people like to lean into. Here's why I think it's so important: Get your colleagues in your head. The ones you've worked alongside for years or the ones you said good morning to today. Every single one of them is in a state of grief or mourning. Every single one has experienced loss. Just like you. It's often invisible as we navigate our days, but just like trauma, grief is something that, if left unacknowledged, will make you pay one way or another. With interest. We are so much more alike than we are different when it comes to grief, as that bitch does not discriminate.

I have moments of amazement that people are able to function as well as they do given the massive, indescribable burden of losing someone they desperately love. If you've buried your baby, your mama, your brother, your best friend, your gido, or your kookum, I see you. I'm so sorry.

In these next few pages, we will set out to define some of the experiences of grief, loss, and mourning. We often equate those words with death. But so many things can mean loss—death, divorce, job loss, friends moving away, a school move, a new sibling. Loss can profoundly impact how we teach and learn, and being armed with some knowledge will help prepare you for when loss occurs in your community.

But first, I want to tell you that I'm writing this from the town where I started college. As I drove here to hide in a hotel room and write, I was struck that it was in this city I met one of my "bottom hands"—one of my most sacred friends, who always caught me when I stumbled. We made many memories in the bar of this hotel (Billy Bob's, for the record). We lived together in residence here. I gave the toast to the bride at her wedding. She helped me rock my twins to sleep. And I gave a tribute to her life at her funeral. She was here for all of *Kids These Days*. In fact, she and her babies helped us send out our first-ever signed copies. And, now, she is no longer on this planet to help with the tears, the triumphs, the challenges, and the dreams that will be *Teachers These Days*. It's a small thing, really, to consider that she won't be a part of what is so important to me when her two babies don't have their mom to celebrate at their graduations or their weddings, for God's sake, and her husband doesn't get to grow old with her. But we had such a story that was ours alone, and sweet Rhea, I am missing you today.

Sometimes, in grief, we get caught up in believing that we don't deserve to feel the way we do. That there must be someone more important who deserves their sadness more. Or when the waves come just as raw as in the beginning, we're shocked that we aren't yet over it. But Rhea reminded me that this discussion is necessary. It's our stories of loss that teach us the most about living. I've told her, many times, in the empty spaces where she used to be, that I would indeed live well for the both of us. I'd like to remind you that you, too, can live well for someone who is not here. You will, without a doubt, be so important for some tiny human or staff member by simply leaning in and living well. We are, after all, together on this journey, walking each other home.

Grief Words: What Do They Mean?

We'll start with a few definitions because understanding these things has changed my life: loss, grief, and mourning. These three words often get mashed together but are deserving of individual clarification, especially if you're the one who will be at the helm when navigating for someone you love, lead, or teach. At any given moment, we're all playing two roles: that of a person who has experienced loss and that of a person supporting someone who has experienced loss.

Loss

Losing someone or something you love is a uniquely individual process. It depends on your experiences and your perception. When we talk about loss in the context of grief, we tend to think mostly about death, such as when we lose a person or animal we love. As teachers, we need to broaden that. Loss will happen to you. It will happen to your students. Grandparents aside, in the United States, 2.5 million children under the age of eighteen have experienced the death of a parent.[1] In Canada in 2011, there were 29,600 foster children who had lost both parents.[2] There are increasing complexities when a student loses a sibling or a loss is due to suicide. And what if you lose a student during the school year?

We can also experience loss when there's a change in routine or when things don't go the way they were supposed to—like divorce or moving to a new school. Or say there was a virus that enveloped the globe and demolished your expectations of walking across the stage to get your diploma. Often our goal is to find the good in the change, the meaning of it all. But we try to jump there too fast and miss the most critical step: the shittiest place of feeling the pain. We skip acknowledging the hurt or how different things are now. Many consider it frivolous to invest this kind of time in loss. Why worry about the things you can't change? It's in line with the "suck it up" mentality that often gets us so messed up in the long run. We don't want to feel it. We often, desperately, want to be over the hardest parts. The goal, my friends, is to not get stuck in this space, which is often why we try to avoid it. Instead, understanding this feeling is a necessary component of healing. Sitting in loss often feels like grief.

Grief

My good friend, funeral director Jeremy Allen, says, "Where loss lives, grief will follow," and this encapsulates much of what we're saying here.[3] Grief is the universal response to loss.[4] You can rarely control this gut response when you lose someone or something, and grief rarely arrives at opportune times. And just when you think you're "fine" or "over it," you hear a song, or smell that campfire, or eat dill pickle chips, and you're brought back to your knees. Grief is much more a feeling or a visceral experience than a thought. I wish there was something you could take to stop grief, or at least suspend it. Turns out, the more you try to avoid it, the more it'll make you pay. It's awful, and painful, and one of the worst things in the human experience.

Grief is also, as many have said, a reflection of love. Dr. Alan Wolfelt says where there was no love, there will be no grief.[5] After Rhea's three-year battle with cancer ended at the tender age of forty-four, I read these words to her and those who loved her at her celebration of life: "There is no grief where there was no love. And if this grief bullshit is any testament to how much I loved you, you were so lucky. And so was I." Because of that love, I mourn her.

Mourning

Mourning is how we heal. The definition of mourning is how you express grief outside of yourself.[6] Grief is an individual process, and often you may want to be alone when it hits. Mourning, on the other hand, tends to be much more connected. Mourning happens in the stories, in saying their name, in laughing and making sense of the hard stuff. Mourning isn't a skill we're born with; it's something we learn how to do by watching others. That's why, dear ones, educators become the safest people to mourn with and are often instrumental in the grief and mourning processes for their students. Remember, something that brings grief to a child will often bring grief to their family. If it's Grandma's death, for example, your student's mom is grieving her mom. Kids don't want to cause more distress to their loved ones, so they may not ask questions at home about what has happened and will happen to Grandma. They may, however, bring those questions to other trusted adults, like their teachers.

Recently, a phenomenal teacher called me to talk through his job of sitting with a group of young men whose friend had attempted suicide. Their friend survived, but the anger, confusion, and continued fear for his safety were immense. This teacher described how they cried, asked questions, and ate all the snacks he brought. It reminded me of the teachers and coaches who sat with me through the most vulnerable times. Teachers didn't sign up for these moments. But I promise you, as I promised him, your students will never forget the space you held for them. Even though the loss in this case was, thankfully, not permanent, those boys needed to mourn what they could have lost, as well as process what they thought they should and could have done, to try to make sense of it.

Mourning tends to be the hardest process to know how to navigate. Oftentimes people don't know what to say or do and have concerns about overstepping boundaries or doing the wrong thing—and rightly so. Emotions are heightened during loss—irritability, anger, and so much sadness. I try to remember, especially in the early stages of grief, that mad is often sad's bodyguard. Mad is generally safer and more accessible, and it keeps people at bay. It's an effective emotion to scare off all the other big emotions that you may not yet have the words for.

We also don't want to make other people sad, so we avoid talking about what was lost. Quite honestly, it's easier to avoid it. We may instead try to make it "fine" and just Mary Poppins the fuck out of it (my new favorite term, by the way). Particularly for people who don't have the emotional language, the very act of talking about hard things becomes debilitating. It's easier to just make like the pain and grief and mourning are not there or not necessary.

Herein lies an important point. Leading in a classroom or staff room often requires emotional language. A school culture where you talk about hard things, like losses within a team or classroom, often comes from those who are able to hold space for the big emotions. That, my friends, is not easy work. There is a cost often not factored into being a connected leader or teacher. (More on this in chapter 7.)

Researchers have repeatedly found that women have been and continue to be better at identifying and naming emotions than men.[7,8,9] This is not because men don't feel emotions but because, despite the fact that we're improving in this area, we still equip our girls with more emotional language than our boys. Society often doesn't let boys express any emotions except for anger. Also problematic is that senior leadership in most every education sector in Canada is still dominated by men, despite the fact that a vast majority of classroom teachers are women.[10,11,12] Regardless of your position in the leadership hierarchy, please know that your contribution to naming the hard things within your school is necessary to create a healthy and connected culture. You can't tell kids how to make sense of the hard things; you have to show them. When the emotion is too much to bear, it may be tempting not to attend a meeting about a school loss because you're "too busy"; however, the anticipatory anxiety is often worse than stepping into the hard stuff. Furthermore, sending/posting/tweeting support is fine, but actually driving to the school or house where a loss happened and showing your face, making eye contact, or bringing food can remarkably influence healing and connection.

Death

Let's talk about death first. Not shying away from asking about the pet, or grandma, or the sibling your student lost is essential. It might not be the best time—and they will let you know—but we often assume that most times are not a good time. Then hours, days, or weeks pass, and we now think it's too late. This quote from Mitch Albom is one of my favorites: "Death ends a life, not a relationship."[13] You can rest assured that people don't forget, particularly, if they've sat in the front row of a funeral service. We're all desperate to know our loved ones won't be forgotten.

Researchers have found that when children's reactions to grief aren't adequately addressed at school, the relationships with their teachers and peers tend to be negatively affected, and that can contribute to poor academic performance.[14] There's much more research on the services and supports provided to students when there's a death in the school family; however, very little attention has been given to the role educators play in grief support. Over the course of their careers, many teachers will have to speak with their students about death; however, many report feeling under- or unequipped to do it.[15,16]

Death of a Student

First of all, for those of you who have walked this journey of losing a student, my heart breaks for you. Losing a student has so many connected layers. There may be siblings within your same school or school system. You often have a relationship with the family, and many teachers are well aware of the relationships the student had with their peers. Some may have had dating relationships or been bullied prior to their death, both of which present significant added complexities.

Every school will have its own response protocols for a student death. I want to talk more generally about things to consider when facing such a loss. First, be sure to connect with your staff. This can feel out of order since we're usually most concerned about creating resources and supports for the children. Checking in with and ensuring your staff are OK first, however, is critically important, because if not, those babes will struggle, too.

Remember that perception is a function of experience. When faced with death, it's often difficult to understand others' reactions—staff and students alike. I've heard stories of teachers who were concerned about the "over-reaction" by students who "barely knew" the child who died or staff who appear to have no visible grief responses. What is remarkable about grief is that it's rarely reflective of just the death at hand. It's often more representative of your body's connection to every other loss you've experienced. After all, "the body keeps the score."[17] It's unlikely you've ever sat at a funeral and not, on some level, reflected on the other times you've been in the same position. Our response may come more from feeling all the losses we've experienced than from a single person or a thing in that moment.

The most important thing you can do is just show up. Fewer words; more listening. You cannot fix it or take it away, so don't try. If you find yourself saying "at least . . .," don't. If witnessing the pain feels unbearable, know that you're right where you need to be. Drop your shoulders. Take a deep breath. Acknowledge it. Then, and only then, can you come up the other side. Start the stories. Remember why they matter. This is never a linear process. Knowing that it comes in waves and that a wave will not last forever is how we survive the storm.

Suicide

Suicide is one of the most horrific words I know. Even as I write it, I get a tightness in my chest. The sheer pain of those considering ending their own life and those left behind continues to be one of the heaviest burdens in this world. If you're navigating the loss of a student or a student's family member by suicide, finding the "right words" feels insurmountable. The desire to fix or make sense of it will be enormous here. It's important, as we've talked about so many times, to first name it. You could say things like, "I wish I knew the right words" or "I wish there was something I could do to make it better." What's more important is to acknowledge that this is heavier than anything, ever.

Sadly, we need to get better in this space, because suicide is far more common than I wish it were. In fact, it is the second-leading cause of death for young people aged fifteen to thirty-four years. The

Center for Suicide Prevention and the Public Health Agency of Canada provide the following information:[18,19]

- Approximately 11 people die by suicide in Canada each day.
- There are approximately 4,000 deaths by suicide per year.
- 1/3 of deaths by suicide are among people 45–59 years.
- Suicide and self-inflicted injuries are the leading causes of death for First Nations youth and adults up to 44 years of age.
- The suicide rate for First Nations male youth (age 15–24) is 126 per 100,000, compared to 24 per 100,000 for non-Indigenous male youth. And suicide rates for Inuit youth are among the highest in the world, at 11 times the national average.

Although your division will have specific protocols for addressing students, staff, and parents post-suicide, here are a few things to consider if you are the teacher who has to share such news.

- It's critical this news be delivered in person, never via announcement system or email. Doing it alongside a staff member who's particularly close to that student cohort can often help with the collecting of emotion.
- Keep connected with those who were closest to the person who died by suicide, as it can be the most vulnerable time and a risk factor for suicidal ideation or completion.
- Of fundamental importance is to remember that you, these kids, and your staff are wired to handle this. Stay connected to each other and your communities as you navigate the days and weeks that follow.
- It's also never too late to connect to the staff, students, and parents who were a part of that person's story. Just as you will never forget that experience, I can assure you, they won't, either.

If you or someone you know is considering suicide, help is available. Call 9-1-1 or

- Kids Help Phone: 1-800-668-6868
  - Text CONNECT to 686868
  - Chat Services [6 pm–2 am EST]: kidshelpphone.ca

- Trans Lifeline: 1-877-330-6366
- Hope for Wellness
  - Help Line: 1-855-242-3310
  - Online chat: hopeforwellness.ca

- Indian Residential Schools Crisis Line: 1-866-925-4419
- Canada Suicide Prevention Service: 1-833-456-4566 [24/7]
- For Quebec residents: [24/7] 1-866-APPELLE

Other Losses

Although we often give the most attention to losses that involve the permanency of death, we can learn to more successfully navigate the loss of other relationships.

Divorce

Although reports on the numbers vary, approximately 40 to 50 percent of all US marriages and almost 49 percent of Canadian marriages will end in divorce.[20,21,22] This means a number of your students may be navigating this significant loss in any given year. As we saw in the previous chapter, divorce is considered one of the top ten adverse childhood experiences; for most kids, divorce is extremely disruptive. Household moves, emotional disconnect from grieving parents, and the sometimes significant discord between parents are also major contributors to emotional dysregulation. All these will filter to the babes, regardless of their age and stage. For the record, my parents divorced during my second year of college, and I have very little memory of that year.

Researchers have also found that divorce and separation correlate positively with diminished school achievement and performance,[23] particularly in the first few months following the marital breakdown.[24] Even with the best lesson plans, kids who are dysregulated cannot learn. As with other losses, acknowledging and holding space are key.

It's also extremely difficult for children when their family relationships aren't healthy. Many of you reading these words may be navigating your own separation or divorce or love someone who is. There is no best time to divorce (i.e., when children are older or younger), and no matter how civil the process, it will be difficult. Lean in to the babies who are experiencing this, particularly in the early days, regardless if they're eight or thirty-eight. Further, give yourself grace if you're the one walking through divorce. What you need is rest, good food, and friends who are heavy on the understanding side and light on the advice side. Stay connected, even if (and especially when) it's the hardest.

Moves

Last but not least, I want to make a brief note about the magnitude of a move in a kid's life. Many kids experience frequent moves. For kids in care, one of the most stressful aspects of starting all over again is walking in the doors of a new school. There's considerable data to suggest that being the new kid can be massively stressful for some children, particularly older ones.[25]

Although circumstances will be different for each student, connection remains your biggest superpower. When you get a new student in your class, try to learn something about them (favorite food, video game, etc.) on their first day, and consider it a huge win if you find common ground in joy. Establishing a connection, any connection, is paramount. Academics should absolutely take a back seat, particularly for kids in care who are navigating so many firsts.

To a lesser extent are disruptions from the expected transitions from elementary to middle school to high school to post-secondary.

Slow down. Notice. Be present. Turns out, the same applies for staff who are new to a school. The integration will happen so much more smoothly. Further, in the madness of this pandemic, there has been so much pressure on teachers to focus on the logistics of educating with a moving target of in-person and/or virtual lessons. Sometimes it is easy to miss the "tells" for when the typical stressors of transitions become overwhelming. There are so many fewer "eyes on" as we navigate these new ways of operating. Taking a few minutes to ask how things are really going can have a huge impact on overall ability to learn and teach.

Teachers Grieve, Too

The majority of the work on grief, loss, and the classroom centers around how we can successfully serve students who are struggling with loss. But again, we know that every one of our colleagues is, right this moment, in some stage of grief and mourning. When a loss occurs in the student population, your teaching team is devastated, too. When you lose a staff member to death, retirement, or a move, the absence can significantly affect a team and the students. I know we forget this all the time, but teachers have a life and relationships outside of the school. They also experience deaths, divorces, miscarriages, and transitions that will require support and space. There's no foolproof series of steps that enables us to perfectly, smoothly, or easily walk someone through the grief process, but don't underestimate just how important you can be in that process.

Those Stages of Grief

Despite the fact that death, grief, and loss are universal, the path through is anything but. Many people go through the stages of grief in some random mixed-up manner. While we can certainly agree that grief is an individual process, there tend to be some common experiences that reflect Elisabeth Kübler-Ross's[26] discussions of grief, including denial, anger, bargaining, depression, and acceptance. David Kessler, Kübler-Ross's protégé, suggested a sixth stage of grief, which he called "meaning."[27] It appears that for those who arrive at a belief that the pain of loss has some larger message or meaning, including finding a way to honor the loss, grief becomes more palatable.

Let's dive into some of the phenomenal work that will happen in those classrooms and staff rooms while navigating loss. Over to you, Mrs. Mac.

My Dad Died

I had a student who would open with, "Hi! My name is Ethan. My dad died." No matter who he met, it was always the same. It was an awkward process to observe. I watched for weeks as every adult he met looked terrified. I would do my best to facilitate the conversation and help both the boy and the obviously uncomfortable adult, but I had no idea whether I was doing or saying the right thing. An amazing human who had recently joined our team as an educational assistant got the "Hi, my dad died" intro, to which she immediately replied, "Thank you so much for sharing. My dad died, too. His name was John. What was your dad's name?" Friends, it took my breath away.

These two taught me so much about grief, loss, and mourning that year. They shared, laughed, cried, and reminisced about their dads. It was an honor to witness. Grief lives in all of us. Just as trauma affects all we do, it's impossible to deny that loss does as well.

Dealing with the Hard Stuff

How can we take care of ourselves in the midst of our own pain? Although no list will suffice, or cover all the bases, we've pulled together a few strategies you can try.

Check It at the Door

My husband, Cody, and I have three babies of our own. I have been pregnant triple that number. Many of those pregnancies ended during the school year. One miscarriage happened the morning I came in to lead a Mother's Day Celebration before heading to the hospital. There's no way I could have just checked my emotions at the door. Not on my first day back, or on an anniversary, or any other day. There's no "forget about life, walk in that door, and teach those babies with a perma-smile on your face." But there are some things I could check as I entered the building that helped me cope and find my way:

1. Where is my breath? Try to get one good breath way down past your chest and into your stomach.
2. Where are my shoulders? Drop them. Feel that stretch and hold it for a few seconds.
3. Do I have a prep today? A break? An "out" if I need it? Find your opportunities for rest.
4. Who's here today? Who can I connect with? Who can help me if and when the grief hits? Find your connections.
5. How will I stay hydrated today? How will I make sure I eat? Will we get a chance for fresh air? Can I find a way to ensure my basic needs are met? Check your own needs.
6. How am I? How will I remind myself that I can do this? If I can't, can I take a day or more to take care of myself? Do I need to be here? Am I pushing myself too far right now doing what's expected and not what I need for my own healing and mental health? Check your emotions.

Check yourself. At the door, in your car, or in your classroom before anyone arrives. This is so tough, but you are tougher.

Who Needs to Know?

We aren't meant to do this whole teaching thing alone, and the same goes for navigating grief or loss. The hardest thing to do when we're in pain is to connect, but it's absolutely essential we do. Let's be clear, not everyone needs to know everything about your story. However, I know that, in my grief, I will need to let others in so I can function, process, and just keep going.

Who needs to know? Who can I rely on and trust to keep my story sacred? Who will not question, judge, or try to fix this for me? Sometimes a list is hard to come by. All you need is one.

David Kessler says:

> Each person's grief is as unique as their fingerprint. But what everyone has in common is that no matter how they grieve, they share a need for their grief to be witnessed. That doesn't mean needing someone to try to lessen it or reframe it for them. The need is for someone to be fully present to the magnitude of their loss without trying to point out the silver lining.[28]

Prepare for the Waves

Grief changes us in ways we can't anticipate. It affects our sleep, appetite, energy, and emotions (and never at convenient times). Every loss we encounter in another person can also trigger memories of a loss of our own. It's not a matter of *if* the waves of grief and loss will hit, it's *when*. Grief is an experience, not just an event. You cannot stop the waves or avoid them all together, but you certainly can brave them. Do you have your life jacket ready? Even a set of water wings will do.

Having some sort of floatation device means you'll be able to stay afloat long enough to acknowledge your feelings instead of avoiding them. It gives you a few moments to plan when you feel like you're going under. It's these moments of preparation when we see that grief can present not only as sadness but anger and guilt as well. It's the time where you get to consider who might be the most skilled—or worthy—to swim alongside you.

I love Shelby Forsythia's words on grief: "It does not get better with time, it gets better with practice."[29] Keep practicing. Or as my girl Dory in *Finding Nemo* says, "Just keep swimming." You will not get over this. You will grieve forever. But it will get better with time.

Say the Name

We know how important language is. We teach it, after all. But some words are just so hard to say. Then there are others we wish no one would ever stop saying. I once had a student whose dog died, and she changed every character's name in every book we read to "Daisy" just so she could speak her name. When we moved to a new city, my son lit up every time his new teacher mentioned Lacombe. When my dad got cancer, I had a hard time telling people what was happening so I would just say, "He's sick," but I longed for people to ask me what kind of sickness so I could say the word "cancer." A student who was part of a shared custody agreement would pray for his mom and dad by name every morning. When a friend's baby passed away, she asked us to consider doing an act of kindness in honor of her precious boy and let the recipient know that it was inspired by Joey.

No matter what the loss entails, using specific names is incredibly powerful. Remember the wonderful educational assistant and student from earlier? The biggest lesson they taught me was to not be afraid to use the names of those we've lost. We all need a safe and comfortable place to say the names of the people, places, and pets we mourn. Let your classrooms be that place.

Celebrate. Together.

Once a kid has been your student, they always have a piece of your heart, and sometimes so do their families. I had a student named Callie whose mother was killed. It was a terrible tragedy, and I was apprehensive about teaching a little one whose trauma and grief were so fresh. That was until I met sweet Callie and her incredible family. They didn't want me to shy away from conversations about the woman they had lost, but to celebrate, remember, and honor her every way we could. In fact, that mama's birthday went on our class calendar. We counted the days like we would for anyone in our little class family. And Callie smiled every time we did. On that birthday, we sang her a big ol' "Happy Birthday"! We welcomed that sweet baby's stories about her mom, including how much she loved the color purple. We looked for purple wherever we could and would often hear a friend say, "Look! There's purple again! Just like your mom loved!" And when we had an occasion with purple balloons and one floated away? Our kids all cheered because Callie's mama was getting a purple balloon in heaven that day.

Celebrate those birthdays and anniversaries. It doesn't have to be an over-the-top, joy-filled, or extravagant experience. But it can be one of quiet grace and dignity for the person who was lost to meet the needs of the one who is mourning.

Ask, Don't Assume

Not every child or family wants and needs their losses to be handled in the same way. Asking, not assuming, is an essential strategy: How would you like me to handle it when he mentions Dad? Is there anything I should let you know about if it comes up in class? Do you use the word "heaven," or "spirit," or "Creator"? Can you tell me more about your loved one? What can I do to help? Asking, not assuming, will help you listen, acknowledge, and hold space for these stories and the kids who share them.

Jim's Story

It was December 1, 2017. The students had some free time at the end of the day. Sam and a group of boys were sitting around Sam's desk playing cards. I was anxious because I was about to head home in a snowstorm.

While my trip was uneventful, it was full of delays. Finally, I made it home, had a late supper, then checked my phone. There were a bunch of messages from my principal, our secretary, and several colleagues. Something was wrong. When I finally reached my principal, I heard these words: "Sam was killed in a farming accident after school today." I was numb.

We met with the trauma team that Sunday and talked about our connections to Sam and his family. When students started arriving, I was waiting for them in my classroom. No one said much, but we knew we needed to be together.

On Tuesday, only five days after their boy had died, Sam's parents asked if they could come into the class. They wanted to see the kids, and they wanted the kids to see them. I was absolutely dreading it because I knew I'd struggle to stay strong and stoic.

When they arrived, Sam's dad stood at the front of the room, sharing memories. He asked the kids to share stories about Sam. Sam's mom went around the room, comforting students who were having a hard time. While we all felt terribly sad, those stories were a huge comfort.

I tried to take my lead from my students. We made a lot of decisions together. Would Sam's locker partner like to switch? What should we do with Sam's desk? We decided to leave everything as it was on Sam's last day. I've heard it said that death is an end of a life, not a relationship. And that is how we got through the rest of our year together. We didn't pretend that he was no longer a part of our lives. In fact, as I reflect on the fact that Sam will always be my student, I am so grateful to him, one of my greatest teachers.

Wrapping Up and Moving On

Grief. Even the sound of that word is harsh. It has hard edges. We don't like to talk about it, but friends, I'm so glad we did, so that you'll know it's acceptable when you feel it or have to face it in your classroom. It's an experience we're all in the middle of to one degree or another, and to heal, we have to give it room to breathe. Let's wrap up your hearts with our three, two, one so you have somewhere to go when the waves hit.

Three things to try

- Reflect on some of the biggest losses you've had as a teacher. Write them down if you're able and just breathe and hold space. You can save the list or burn it, but make sure to acknowledge how many stories you've been a part of.

- If there's been a loss this year in your course, classroom, or staff room, don't be scared to say their name. Ask about the loss and notice the responses—yours and theirs.

- Think about someone you've lost—maybe the one who is heaviest on your heart today (and that can change, by the way). What could you do to honor or celebrate them? Remember, this death thing ends a life, not all that life meant to you.

Two quotes to consider

"Grief is in two parts. The first is loss. The second is the remaking of life." —Anne Roiphe

"How lucky am I to have something that makes saying goodbye so hard."—Winnie-the-Pooh

One question to answer

- What has been the most valuable experience or practice you've been a part of as your team (past or present) has navigated a loss in a school or class?

6

Reconnection: What Works and What Doesn't

I've had the privilege of working with amazing teachers and speaking to many different groups from so many walks of life. Whether it's funeral directors, bus drivers, physicians, Indigenous Elders, 4-H leaders, or minor league hockey coaches, the foundation of my talk is the same. I use largely the same slides and similar videos. Although my stories change, the truth about relationship and connection transcends culture and profession. In this chapter, we'll take it down to five foundations of connection and reconnection that teachers these days can depend on.

Before we talk about what does work, I want to talk about two things often done in education that I think are not working: out-of-school suspensions and individual program plans (IPPs).

What Doesn't Work

If our goal is a relationship-focused, trauma-informed school, we must address these two things. As we've established, the emotional regulation of our students must take precedence. If people, including your students, are seen, acknowledged, and understood, they will rise. They will learn from their mistakes. They'll benefit from consequences (when necessary). They'll want to be better. They will be able to learn the curriculum to the best of their cognitive ability. If policy and procedure are enforced without this fundamental understanding, we will not serve kids in the relational shift that is necessary. Our distance from one another will continue to grow and disconnection will prevail.

Grace Murray Hopper, one of the first female computer programmers and a US Navy rear admiral, said, "The most dangerous phrase in the language is 'We've always done it this way.'"[1] When I spend time with educators, I often wonder about the approach to emotional dysregulation in schools. At the heart of this question is, how is "bad behavior" responded to? Let's not forget that underlying all bad behavior is emotional dysregulation, which is an attempt to seek connection in the most unlikely and often inappropriate ways, in many cases ways that are hurtful and sometimes illegal. With that in mind, how is your district or school responding to your most significant connection-seekers? What is the philosophy behind disciplinary practices?

Suspensions Are a Pipeline to Prison

Historically, particularly when approaching emotional dysregulation from a behavioral perspective, we have attempted to punish bad behavior, hoping it will make kids "snap out of it" and understand that their nice peers who make good choices get treated better. The more dysregulated or violent kids become, the more ill-equipped we often feel to assist, teach, and stay present with them. What happens when we feel ill-equipped? Generally, our lid flips and we go into fight-or-flight mode ourselves. We want to fix it. We want an answer. We want compliance. And we want to remove the threat so we can return to a sense of calm. So, we remove the "bad kids" as the ultimate form of punishment. Originally, another intention of suspension measures was to withdraw the disruptive children so as not to impact those who are "ready to learn." Interestingly, the data do not support this.[2]

It is necessary to have take-charge policies and procedures built into our institutions for when people are out of control and need a break or need to be kept safe. School officials often have considerable discretion over discipline policy, and when they lean toward harsher discipline, it has negative long-term impacts on students.[3] If we're truly committed to creating trauma-informed schools, out-of-school suspensions need to be seriously reviewed. Suspension policies are antiquated and harmful if they don't include plans for a supportive re-entry and if there are no efforts to stay connected to the student during the suspension or to prepare other students for their return.

The discussion around exclusionary disciplinary policies, specifically zero-tolerance policies that remove students from the school environment, is not new. The prevailing concern is that this practice can increase the probability of a youth coming into contact with the incarceration system. In 2005, the NAACP issued this statement:

> In the last decade, the punitive and overzealous tools and approaches of the modern criminal justice system have seeped into our schools, serving to remove children from mainstream educational environments and funnel them onto a one-way path toward prison. . . . The School-to-Prison Pipeline is one of the most urgent challenges in education today.[4]

Researchers also report that out-of-school suspension increases referrals to the juvenile justice system among youth with a history of offending behaviors.[5] Schools vary widely in the number of suspensions handed out, and sometimes districts aren't even required to report suspension rates,[6] but students who attended schools with higher suspension rates are reported to be 15 to 20 percent more likely to be arrested and incarcerated as adults.[7] Punishment and school-related arrests show that the racial disparity begins the school-to-prison pipeline. Further, the negative impacts of attending a high-suspension school are largest for male and marginalized students. In Ontario, researchers reported that 18 percent of white students reported at least one school suspension before graduation, whereas 42 percent of Black students in the same cohort reported at least one suspension. Further, Black students often attend schools with less-qualified, less-experienced teachers who receive lower salaries, and underfunded schools with large Black populations are more likely to employ zero-tolerance policies.[8]

We've long subscribed to the idea that we have to set an example of what it looks like to follow rules. That we can't let students "get away with" disrespectful or unacceptable behavior. We have to "make an example" of the ones who don't fall in line so that others will learn. I'd like to suggest that the opposite is true. See, kids are watching all the time. Their job is to mess up, and our job is to show them how to have hard conversations and handle hard situations. To work through differences. To seek first to understand before being understood.[9] One of the biggest questions we can ask ourselves is, "How do the big people respond to the little(r) people who struggle the most?" One of the first steps will be to identify whether in- and out-of-school suspension rates are documented in your respective division.

The Motivators and the Triggers IEP

Since we're going for the jugular, we might as well go all in, my friends. Here's the other thing that commonly happens in classrooms that needs our immediate attention: individual education plans (IEPs), sometimes called individual program plans (IPPs).

Originally, IEPs were developed to address students who need extra educational support within the classroom. Learning difficulties are often paired with frustration and emotional dysregulation, which has led to many IEPs that focus, specifically, on behavioral concerns. This worries me greatly, especially when the primary focus is on creating a list of motivators and triggers to manage these concerns, with little (or no) consideration of the context in which these behaviors occur. As we've established, if you have a big enough stick (i.e., motivator), you can get most people to do most anything. The question should be more about *why* a kid is doing what they are doing. If there are triggers, or things that set them off, what's the story? Why do they respond so significantly to male teachers or loud noises? And let's challenge the idea that when we take away the things kids love, they have to earn them back. At the heart of every support plan should be the child's story and a focus on emotional regulation. Then, and only then, can we build in the structures they will need to stay on track.

As teacher and inclusion expert Shelley Moore explains, although IEPs were intended to support students with needs within a classroom, they are often long, difficult to understand, exclusionary for students with significant needs, left to an educational assistant to carry out, and don't align with curriculum, Moore's book *All for One: Designing Individual Education Plans for Inclusive Classrooms* is one of the best resources we have seen on the subject. She eloquently addresses the importance of creating IEPs that are universally inclusive to all students and discusses the critical importance of designing plans that are easy for educators *and* parents to follow. She encourages us to consider both the student's and classroom's entire story so they can grow together.[10]

Many institutions have done significant work in this regard, while others have a long way to go. We need to ask: What's the end goal? Is it working? When making IEPs, we can ask why the behavior is occurring, not necessarily how concerning the behavior itself is. Specific rules and policies can differ, depending on region or resources, but it's important to know what drives the practices within your building. Let the understanding that safety is paramount and that, whenever possible, connection must occur before direction be the foundation that guides you. This philosophy will be reflected in your teams and to the students who will grow for the better just for being a part of it.

If It Were Just That Easy

Wouldn't it be amazing if we could have a list of steps that would lead to emotional regulation in schools? And to regulated staff standing ready to help re-regulate any kid in need? And if these steps addressed bias, trauma, grief, and our own histories, while taking into account the realities we face as those charged with walking little (and sometimes big) humans home? Although I don't think "the answer" exists to anything in this life, I do believe that the five keys to reconnecting are a solid starting point.

The Five Keys to Reconnecting

It's easy to point out the things that don't work, but now we're going to talk about the things that do work. Every time. See, our biggest job is in the creation of corrective experiences, especially when limits or boundaries are required. These five strategies are meant to help guide the underlying philosophical practice, for both you and the culture in which you serve.

Key 1: Show Genuine Interest in the Things They Care About

The single word that best captures this first strategy is "acknowledgment." Oh, the power of that one little word! If I'm going to walk someone through a hard morning, or if I see cut marks on a student's wrist, or if I'm worried about a colleague who is driving me around the bend, the superpower I need is the simple strategy coined by Dan Siegel: you have to "name it to tame it."[11]

When we're acknowledged for the things we like or don't, for our story, for how difficult or exciting something is in a given moment, we warm toward that, like sunshine. We're more likely to take direction from, listen to, and learn from someone who sees us. This genuine interest is the foundation to empathy.

Although the word "empathy" gets thrown around often, at its core, it simply means, without judgment, attempting to imagine what it might be like to experience what another is feeling.[12] The "without judgment" part is nearly impossible for many of us. It takes skill to step out of your shoes and into another's, if even for a brief moment. It's not about condoning, or supporting, or even understanding why someone does or believes as they do, but rather about demonstrating your efforts to understand them. You're not born with this skill. In fact, the only way we build this muscle is when people give us empathy and we practice and practice it. I've had many conversations over the years with big people who are concerned that the little people they're assessing or teaching don't have empathy. The assumption is that there's something to fear because of this supposed massive deficit. But, unless someone has suspended judgment and really tried to understand what it's like to be you, you cannot do that for another.

When explaining the power of key 1, I often refer to the idea of holding space—trying, for as long as humanly possible, to not offer strategies or solutions. Fair warning, this might be the hardest thing you've ever been called to do as a teacher: to not fix. Without question, this is the most significant feedback I've received as a therapist: Don't fix. Just hold space. And I, my friends, am a fixer. Not a slow, methodical, make-sure-we've-measured-everything-twice kind of fixer, either. So, I've had to borrow a few insights from some of the greats as I, too, continue to learn to hold space and not jump to fix. Here are the top three phrases I use:

- "Tell me more."
- "What's the hardest part?"
- "What am I missing?"

In *Kids These Days*, I wrote that learning from kids will be your best bet for connection. The latest TikTok challenge? Hottest music? Ask them. Number one YouTuber? What's it mean to be pansexual? They'll know it. Don't try to pretend you know if you don't. Let's not kid ourselves—although you still look like you're seventeen, a lot has changed since then, my friend. Also, for the record, this key also works beautifully with your colleagues, and they likely need to be seen just as much as those students.

Key 2: Get Their Eyes and Say Their Names

This has got to be my favorite (and you know that's a big deal because food trumps most things for this Ukrainian girl—see key 4). Even if you have a mask on or you're behind a screen, smiling with your eyeballs has never been more important. Your ability to connect with other human beings is your calling card, and so much of that happens with not only looking but seeing. For example, some kids are figuring out their gender identity or may simply prefer to be called something other than what's in their record. Do you know your students' correct names and their pronouns?

Once you know their names, make sure you say them, but also make sure you know *how* to say them. Sarah Adomako-Ansah is a teacher and co-founder of the Black Teachers Association of Alberta. She told me that many of her sixth-grade students struggle to say her name properly, so she encouraged them to call her "Ms. A." When her students absorbed the importance of being seen—truly having people know who they are, how their name sounds, what it's like to hear their name pronounced correctly—Ms. A received a message from a student. It read: "Dear Ms. Adomako-Ansah, I have called you Ms. A forever, because it was easier for me. After learning from you, it was clear to me that if we can say 'Tchaikovsky' correctly, surely we can learn the name of the woman who works so hard to teach us every day. So, from now on, you will be 'Ms. Adomako-Ansah' to me."

We can have diverse teams, made up of different races, cultures, experiences, ages, and gender identities; however, to truly be inclusive, we have to recognize the immeasurable contributions such a team can offer, letting them talk while the rest of us listen. What do they bring to your group? Do you know how to say the names of everyone who sits with you? Our name is the first word we learn, and we know how it's supposed to sound.[13] When people get it right, and particularly if they don't, it can mean everything.

Key 3: Get Down on Their Level

Get on your bum in the boot room. Stand at the front of the lecture hall when your students file in hungover and smile at each one. Sit side by side on the bench after the basketball game. If you're having virtual meetings with your students, staff, or parents, have your camera on and situated at eye level. They need to see you, especially if you're interacting virtually. The anonymity of texts or even emails can sometimes lead to fight or flight taking over. (Ever wonder why Trump was a Twitter fan and not Instagram? Twitter is far more anonymous than other social media platforms.) There are, of course, privacy issues that can come into play for your students, and they have a right to that. The importance is in the continued engagement and requests to connect. If I can see you, I'm much more inclined to slow down, regulate, and be thoughtful and purposeful. That matters when we're talking about important things, like relationships that have ruptured or grades that need to improve.

Key 4: Feed Them and They Will Come

This little gem here is and will remain the secret 007 trick. Your grandmother knew about it, and we eventually figured it out, too: you can't chew and swallow with a flipped lid. It's biologically impossible because you would choke. We have historically used food as a reward, and we lost a lot of ground when someone decided that a good snack needs to be earned. If you want to watch a little magic in action, notice what happens when you get a kid to take a sip of water or eat a few Goldfish crackers when they're having a hard time. Having a coffee while talking with a student about their grades can, indeed, change the conversation. Here's another tip for free: you can't regulate a kid with a carrot stick. Treats are a must. For you and them. Have you ever nursed a broken heart with a salad?

After talking about using food and drink not as a reward but as a regulation strategy, a teacher asked me if I was "worried about contributing to the obesity epidemic."

No. No, I am not.

I know we worry we might set a dangerous precedent by allowing tools like food into our classroom (mindful of allergies and food sensitivities). But I promise you will not. Stop being scared of what could go wrong, and start thinking about how listening to student needs and addressing them and providing students with access to the tools necessary to regulate and learn will feel.

If you regulate a student with food or a drink, the other kids won't flip their lids just to get a piece of gum like the other kid has. Being in a state of lid-flip is not where anyone wants to be. It may be true that other kids might ask about getting one, too; however, if their lid is on, you have the discussion that different people need different things at different times, which will be one of the most significant lessons you'll teach that day. So what if the regulated kids get a cookie or a snack break? Remember that food nourishes the mind as well as the body.

Once we get that lid back on (you'll know if there's a deep sigh or they've swallowed their juice), then you will be able to truly teach, talk about consequences (if necessary), impart your wisdom, change lives. Because now they can hear you. This two-step process of regulating first isn't where you stop. The teaching of the lesson, the trying it again, is critical. If a kid isn't interested in having a snack, you need to dial it back. I know you're desperate to get the lesson in, but that student is not yet ready.

Key 5: Never Leave Them

You've heard me say it before and I'll say it again: we are wired for connection. We're desperate to reconnect once a connection has been ruptured (hence, the upcoming chapter on repair). We know, intuitively, that we're not meant to do this alone. This whole human existence thing is a contact sport. There are times when we need our independence and space. Time-outs are such a good thing—for you, not them. Consider what we think happens during time-outs—"Go to your room, then reflect on your sins and remember how lucky you are"—versus what actually happens. Epiphanies, friends, don't often happen when kids are sent into hallways or to the office, alienated from the others. Sometimes, they may decide that the consequence is a big enough motivator to have their lid slammed back on, but what skill did we teach this kid? What they now understand is that if you make someone scared enough, they will comply. What we want is to show them how to co-regulate and work through the hard things, so eventually they can do that for themselves and then other people as they grow. Once again, you can't give away something you've never received.

Another powerful thing that requires proximity is the healing force of laughter. And not the shaming, jokey kind; I mean the belly-jiggling, doubled-over kind. I can tell you that the quickest assessment of school or university culture is the amount of joy you hear in the hallways. Laughter brings with it a release of oxytocin, the feel-good hormone, and a necessary movement through stressful responses.[14,15] Sometimes, with so much on the docket in a school day, when you're holding the emotions of so many souls, there's little room for reprieve. Even reminiscing about something that cracked your staff up works to shift your prefrontal cortex back into the present and inject a little well-deserved shot of resilience.

The other magic-maker that often requires proximity is physical contact. Now, in the middle of a global pandemic, I get that you might not be pulling the FedEx guy in for a bear hug, but know that there's power in contact. The research is clear: a six-second kiss or a twenty-second hug changes your neurochemistry; it also releases oxytocin. While throwing your lips around on school property is likely not in your best interest, think about intentionally leaning on the people you love the most daily.

This Is How We Do It

Cue the Montell Jordan song. And there you have it—these five keys transcend age, race, religion, and gender identity. Now, Mrs. Mac's going to talk about them as they might apply to your students and staff.

How the Five Keys Apply to Us All

Regulation takes precedence, and it's our job to show, not tell, students how this can be done. Turns out, even the best teachers out there experience disrespect, eye rolls, and losing-their-minds behaviors, not because they can't manage children, but because their students are figuring out the necessary skill of learning to regulate. No regulation equals no learning. Who could argue with that?

But it can be so stinking hard to not only remember it but to live it. Our systems have been set up in ways that often don't support diverse needs and identities nor the need for teaching and assisting emotional regulation. And it's damn hard to do this if we don't feel supported by our school or district.

We never arrive at a perfectly shifted culture. We are always in the process of building a better one. And this process isn't solitary. Surround yourself with people who are also working toward shifting a culture one step at a time. If you've got a village of on-the-same-pagers in your institution right now, let's go! If you feel like no one else yet sees the promised land, just start with the closest believer. Find one person to lean on. No one in your building? That's no longer a problem in this technologically connected world. Find someone in your community or even on social media who understands the time and effort you put into regulation work.

We think the five keys are foolproof strategies when applied to students as well as colleagues. Let's see how we can use each one to reconnect with our kids and colleagues—the army of culture shifters we are fixing to create.

The Five Keys in the Classroom

Key 1: Show Genuine Interest in Our Kids

A mom who was considering putting her son in our class midway through the year came for a school tour. I gave her our information and smiled and tried to reassure her that he would be welcomed and valued. She still looked uneasy. I asked, "What questions do you have about him joining our class?"

Her response: "Do you have any farm toys?"

I explained that we did and that the kids loved to play with them. She breathed a huge sigh of relief and told me that there was nothing her son loved more than farms, but his previous teacher had taken the farm toys away when she deemed him "too obsessed with farms" and determined he would find other interests.

I promised her that, in my class, he would be able to play with the farm toys, and play with the farm toys he did. Often those toys helped him build relationships with others through play and to express his emotions when his words would not come. This wasn't the time to expand his passions or take his favorite toys. This was the time to let him shine in all his farm-loving glory and to take interest in that love.

What "farm toys" are you going to keep on the table? Video games? JoJo Siwa? Gathering information about and making your students' interests part of their world at school instead of expecting them to shut them off gives them a voice and choice. Remember: You don't necessarily condone any of these interests. Your job is simply to seek first to understand.

Showing Genuine Interest in Our Colleagues

Think of three colleagues right now. Not your teacher besties. That's too easy. I'm talking about three people you may cross paths with in the hall or sit near during the occasional meeting but would like to connect with more.

Now, do a little mental inventory of what you know about each of them. Which car in the parking lot is theirs? Do they live with anyone?

Where did they grow up? Do they have pets, children, significant others? Let's start even simpler: What are their names? Do you know how to pronounce them? Do you know their coffee orders? Whether you know the answers or not is irrelevant at this point. If anyone immediately popped in your head, that is where you start.

Time is always our rarest commodity. Do the best you can with what you've got. Try to learn just a little more. It will bring so much to the reconnection table.

Key 2: Get Their Eyes and Say Their Names

Every day in one particular course (EDU 305 if I remember correctly), my professor said good morning to a hoodie-clad student. I noticed the interaction, first, because I was shocked that the student didn't respond. They avoided eye contact. And, every time, I noticed that the prof carried on with no attempt to bring attention to the apparent disrespect. I started to watch for it. I wanted to know if he was going to give up. Or if this student was going to stop coming. And then it happened. Maybe two months in, the kid looked up and simply grumbled, "Morning." No one else heard it, except the prof. In the social psych experiment in my head, I was glued to this exchange. The response was brilliant and oh-so-subtle. I saw the prof turn his back to the lecture hall and give a very subtle fist pump. I never put it together then, but what I take from it now had nothing to do with the course outline.

It can take time. It can feel futile and tricky because, as we know, you rarely get the connection thing right all the time. Slow down and get to know your student's light-up style. Are they big and bold like me? Or low and slow like the dude in my class?

Dale Carnegie said, "A person's name is to him or her the sweetest and most important sound in any language."[16] I fell in love with my husband when he ended a date by looking at me and saying, "Goodnight, Laurie." I've joked that, had he not said my name that day and in all of our phone calls as a long-distance couple, we might not be where we are today. Hearing him say my name instantly grounds me. I know the peace it brings me to hear my name from someone I trust, and I strive to do that for the kids I serve.

Typically, many of us are better with the kids than with our colleagues. Does this strategy work for the big people, too? Oh, you know it's true. I teach our kids that when someone comes into our classroom, we greet them with our eyes (look at them), our hand (give a friendly wave), and our mouth (say something welcoming, preferably adding their name to up the connection ante). Yet, when I made my list of three staff members I'd like to connect with, that task suddenly seemed hard. Can I walk past them in the hallway and do these three vulnerable things? Acknowledging is a connection superpower. And don't forget this tricky truth: the hardest ones to give it to are the ones who need it most.

We know that some people are easier to give to than others. From four-year-olds to adults, I have had people grumble and groan, walking right past me as I do my best light-up. Brainstorm ways you can continue to connect with the people in your life. Choose something you're comfortable with, such as a chat in the staff room to ask about their upcoming plans for the weekend. Could you write them a quick thank-you card explaining why your school community is lucky to have them? How about sharing a coffee or tea to start the week?

Key 3: Get on the Kids' Level

Getting on the floor with our learners (especially mid-lid-flip) is one of the most powerful tools we have as teachers. Sitting beside them, at eye level, is an important way to just be with them. For the big kids, it sometimes requires us to ask them to sit beside us.

Terri's Story

I had no formal training as an educational assistant when I was hired to work with a little one in grade two. He peed himself daily, threw anything he could, ran away from staff, spat, swore, hit, kicked. You name it.

On my first day with him, he ran. I knew I had a choice to make. I sat down in the middle of the hall and calmly said I'd wait right there until he was ready to come back. He stopped in his tracks. He was used to everyone chasing him. He came back and wanted to talk about it. I knew he wanted connection.

I became his biggest cheerleader. I would ask him to leave the room with me for breaks before he would flip his lid. We'd go fly a kite, draw on the sidewalk, read in the library, anything that let us do side-by-side activities together and build connection. By the end of the year, he was still calling me a "stupid fucking cow," but he came to school every day. I kept track and showed the whole team: he was spending more time in the classroom than out. That side-by-side connection was key.

Get on Your Colleagues' Level

How do you "get down" with your colleagues? Let me start with a story about my friend, Claire, who was struggling with a colleague. As a new teacher, Claire would call me crying about a teacher would come to her class about once a week, sit on her counter, and talk with her about something she had done "wrong." Claire was finding it hard to participate in these conversations. I asked her what she needed in order to be able to "hear" the information this teacher was trying to give her. She said, "I just wish they'd get off my damn counter! I feel like they're looking down at me literally AND figuratively!" It wasn't that Claire wasn't open to feedback; she just wasn't able to process that feedback in the way it was presented. The act of the teacher sitting on the counter instead of next to her made all the difference. Be sure to be on the same level as your colleagues, especially in those tough conversations when you want to connect.

Key 4: Feed the Children

I have a small bin hidden away with gum, mints, drinks, and crunchy snacks (for those who need the hard snap of a food in the midst of their lid-flip). I've found that being prepared helps me keep my own lid on in the situation. The bin is close by so I don't need to go running to find things. It's always ready to go.

I talk with my students about how everyone's needs are different and that's OK. We have these talks frequently throughout the year so they not only know that I'm open to all types of tools to help us regulate but also that I have their backs in case they need it. I want them to know that, despite their mood or mindset or mistakes, they are valued and will be taken care of. If food or drink gets that message across, I'm happy to use it.

Halee wrote to us with a story about Starburst candy, and I literally went out and bought a Costco-sized bag for my bin of goodies.

Halee's Story

One day, during math, we were working on a review. One student came across a hard question and, after trying and failing a few times, had a total lid-flip moment. Ripped papers, kicked chairs, shoved desks, crying, and flailing on the floor. I immediately grabbed a Starburst (his favorite) and went to sit down on the floor right next to him. I gave him the Starburst. I had one, too. We chewed. We took a deep breath. And I sat right there with him until he was done. Some days we dance. Some days we cry on the floor. But Starbursts are always magic.

Feed Your Colleagues

My very favorite way to treat colleagues is with a morning coffee. A colleague at our school had the brilliant idea of creating a shared Google doc with everyone's coffee preferences, and I can't even tell you how wonderful this has been. Instead of buying for the same few people whose orders I know by heart, I often find myself in the drive-through checking the document to order for someone who is having a rough week and needs a pick-me-up.

Keep some emergency snacks in your room for those after-school teacher vents, too. Being able to offer a soda or piece of candy during an "I can't freaking do this anymore" teacher meltdown will help you and your colleagues keep your lids on as you reflect on the good days and the bad.

As Giada De Laurentiis said, "Food brings people together on many levels. It's nourishment of the soul and body; it's truly love." Isn't that the truth? If you're part of a team that's dysregulated, connection will be a struggle, but food can help.

Key 5: Proximity with Our Learners

Aaron Hogan, author of *Shattering the Perfect Teacher Myth*, is one of my all-time favorite people. He writes, "When students can't read, we teach them. When students can't write, we teach them. So when students can't behave, why do they get put in the hall?"[17] Lightbulb moment! Proximity is not only a connection builder, it's also a dignity maintainer.

I was sent out of the classroom one time as a kid. Once. And I can still feel the shame and the embarrassment to this day. Remember, a lid-flip is your cue that this human is under too much stress. Putting them in the hallway alone or in a time-out spot in a corner is only going to contribute to that stress. If it's you who needs a break, first, get someone who's able to stay with the class so they don't feel isolated or alone, then take your break and get your lid back on. Our kids shouldn't be made to feel as though they're walking alone during a lid-flip or times of grief.

Daniele's Story

When I was in grade two, I lost my dad in a farm accident. My mom was also seven months pregnant with her fifth baby, so I'm sure her plate was pretty full. In one corner of the room, my amazing, beautiful teacher, Lorraine, made a special hideout for me with divider panels and filled it full of pillows and blankets and stuffed animals and books. She told me I could go in there whenever I wanted; I didn't have to ask first, and no one else was allowed in without my permission. She bought me *The Chronicles of Narnia* because she knew how much I loved to read. I don't remember much about that time in my life, but I remember what she did for me. She gave me space to grieve.

In the room where she knew the smells, and the sounds, and the stories, she was allowed to make sense of the hard stuff. Keep 'em close even if they say, "Go away." Give them space, but keep checking back.

Proximity with Our Colleagues

A team without joy will not function well. When we're able to live and work where we're all fighting for the same, we'll remember that we're more alike than different, and then we can make magic happen together.

This is why it's so critical to find joy with your team, so that collectively you're all working for the same purpose: to walk those kids home. Need some inspiration? Share the memory of something ridiculous that happened in your building. A funny sign in the mug cupboard. A surprise in someone's mailbox. A planned staff dress-up day to delight your learners. Whip out your microphones for an epic karaoke showdown in the hallway. You can do this.

Proximity with our colleagues also brings us back to the notion of holding space. So, on the days when it *is* just *too* much? When that teacher across the hall comes in crying because they just can't take one more day of this? Hold. That. Space. No awfulizing. No advice. No "good vibes only" rhetoric. Just be there for them and they will, in turn, be there for you.

We will end this chapter with a beautiful story we received that reminded us of what can happen when an entire staff understands the five keys and uses them together:

Justin's Story

Justin was in the middle of a giant lid-flip. He was slamming doors in the bathroom, screaming obscenities at adults, and running from spot to spot throughout the building. Adults from around the school came when they heard the screaming and slamming. As they showed up, I realized they didn't show up to punish or shame, but to be the bottom hands for Justin and for the adults who were trying to support him.

As Justin shoved past me, called me an asshole, and sprinted to the library, another teacher came up beside me, and we walked together to the library. He checked in with me, spoke calmly, and helped me catch my breath and even chuckle. He was my bottom hands.

When we arrived at the library, Justin was under a table screaming "FUCK" at any passerby. Five adults gathered, not circling or trapping him. They were there to offer lifelines of connection, as we had all been building relationships with Justin for months. We gathered in a loose circle around where Justin had hidden under the table, with four adults standing and one sitting on the floor within his eyesight. We talked about our plans for the weekend. We talked about a space documentary we had seen. (Justin loved space.) We talked about our pets. (Justin was most at peace talking about his pets.) We modeled calm voices and deep breaths.

Slowly, Justin shifted from yelling and swearing to listening, then inserting himself in the conversation. One of the teachers mentioned he was doing a lesson on space after recess. Justin asked if he could join that class for the lesson. All the while, he slowly caught his breath and began to edge out from under the table. He saw he was safe, felt the connection, and knew he was part of a relationship with grown-ups who cared about him—and who knew how to be his bottom hands.

To stand in a circle with calm grown-ups surrounding a struggling child who needed connection and calm, to trust that every adult in the circle knew why we weren't yelling, why we weren't consequencing, and why we were going to give him a dignified exit strategy . . . that is what it means to understand and be understood. That is what it means to stand in a circle with the winners. That is what it means to support our children—especially the ones who need it in the loudest, messiest ways.

Of course, keeping each other and our kids and families safe is paramount. Take-charge moments are sometimes necessary. But it's usually when we're employing the five keys that our legacies are being laid, cycles are being broken, corrective experiences are being had, and lives are being changed.

Wrapping Up and Moving On

If only we could have all the answers. If only these strategies *were* always those answers. Unfortunately, that's not the case, but we know in our hearts that the five keys do work when the time is right. There are so many times when connecting, lighting up, and just having a snack is the way home. There will be times when we mess it up—that's why the next chapter is all about repair—but here's our three, two, one to tuck into your coat for those particularly rainy days.

Three things to try

- Make a list of three colleagues to connect—or reconnect—with over the next weeks and months. Notice what happens.
- Make a coffee/tea order Google doc. You don't necessarily have to use it, but creating it will be meaningful to all who are included. Remember, it's not about spending money on someone else; it's about connecting and showing them they are seen.
- Video chat (not text or email) with someone you haven't seen for some time. Don't worry about your hair. You look great. They need to see you. And you need to see them.

Two quotes to consider

"I define connection as the energy that exists between people when they feel seen, heard, and valued; when they can give and receive without judgment; and when they derive sustenance and strength from the relationship." —Dr. Brené Brown

"Every person was born with a set of spiritual instructions or understandings, my girl. It's what we do with it that defines us as human beings." —Aimee Craft

One question to answer

- Think about the kid whose trajectory you truly changed. You might not have received a tangible accolade, but how did you know? Sit with that feeling, amazing one.

7

Repairing the Ruptured Relationships

This is the chapter we needed to write the most. Know why? Because we're going to fuck it up. We will forget our "why" once in a while. We will flip our own personal lids. We will do and say things that felt completely justified in the moment (and maybe even out of the moment) but will require the skillful art of repair. Apologies—repairing an inevitable disconnect—are by far the most important ingredient for human connection. Like so many things, we are not born with the skills to fix a broken connection. We have to be shown how to do it. To learn to give an apology, we have to receive them first. Many times. Only then will we have the necessary neural pathways to formulate a reparative response.

There are two things to consider when things start to break down in this holy work. First, how do we attend to ruptured relationships to get them back on track? And, second, what do we do when we're too tired to carry the responsibility that comes with teaching, especially when burnout takes over?

Repairing Relationships

Clinical psychologist Harriet Lerner is a powerhouse in the world of repair. One of the most respected voices in the world of women and psychology, she has been studying apologies for over two decades. Her books sit with dog-ears and worn spines on my shelf. Her most recent book, *Why Won't You Apologize?*, is profound.[1] It tells us just what we need to know to raise people who understand the importance of a heartfelt apology. Equally critical is the damage a bad apology can cause. If you haven't experienced sincere apologies enough, you won't be able to give them away.

How many times has someone held your gaze and said, "I'm sorry," and you believed they meant it? Not only is it hard to give a sincere apology, it's also incredibly difficult to receive one. Think about those students in your class who are struggling the most. How often do you think the big people in their lives have apologized to them? The healing power of a good apology is immediately recognizable. Anger and resentment often melt away.

Here's the deal: You will need to apologize to the kids you teach. You will need to apologize to your colleagues. You will need to apologize to your children (if you have them) and your partner (if you have one)—this is especially important if you have a former partner with whom you share children.

A good apology will never contain the words "but" or "if." Those qualifiers erase the apology. Reflect on the times you've done something you know you need to atone for, but you just couldn't help sneaking in a teachable moment at the end. That's where you lose your power. When you said, "Honey, I'm sorry I was so bitchy when I came home last night, *but* if you'd just gotten dinner started . . ." Or, "Kids, Daddy is really sorry for yelling, *but* if you'd just pick up your toys . . ." Every damn time those words sneak through your lips, you erase all the good work of a genuine apology.

This is also not an apology: "I'm sorry you're so sensitive" or "I'm sorry you feel that way." We may think we're being kind when we say those words, but it's actually a subtle form of gaslighting.[2] You may be right—they may be sensitive or misguided; however, if your goal is to repair the relationship rather than shame the other person, the focus has to be on your actions, not theirs.

Genuine apologies also spend very little time unpacking who is to blame. Sometimes it's important to get the facts; however, the facts are hard to decipher when lids are flipped. Pinpointing who is more justified or correct seldom results in the other party accepting fault. It needs to be about being heard, not who is most right (a tricky one for us competitive types).

A genuine apology is also backed by corrective action—you have to change the behavior or attempt to do better. If you go on to repeat the disservice after issuing an apology, it becomes very difficult to trust that apology. The goal is to demonstrate sincerity—you can't just tell someone you're sorry; you have to show them. Further, we tend to think that once we've apologized, the other person should be over it. But an apology isn't an instantaneous cure. Sometimes the magic lies in our willingness to sit in the mess while an apology takes hold.

Apologies are exhausting, but some of the most important lessons you will ever teach will be centered around repair. People who have the most difficulty regulating emotion have rarely experienced genuine repair. Instead, they've had people attempt to fix their behavior or suggest ways they could be different or better. Although these points can be valid and maybe even warranted, the collecting power found in a sincere apology is the mark of great leaders. It will lead to growth much more quickly. Use accordingly and often.

Repairing When Burnout Sets In

If you're burned out, you will have a hard time showing anyone how to do anything, including how to repair. Burnout was a term coined in 1974 by psychologist Herbert Freudenberger,[3] who was one of the first to describe the consequences of severe stress and "high ideals" at work. Burnout, he said, has three components:

1. Emotional exhaustion (think tiredness in your bones)

2. Depersonalization (losing empathy and compassion)
3. Decreased sense of accomplishment (everything feels futile)

When I first started researching burnout, I was working on the inpatient unit at the Alberta Children's Hospital. Those first few years, I often felt in over my head, like I wasn't qualified to be there, while at the same time feeling responsible for all of it. I found myself staying long hours just to make sure kids were settled into bed, and I wrote reports every weekend. I felt perpetually resentful of all the work that was expected of me, which so often felt futile. How was this going to work if I was already losing compassion? How could I be an effective psychologist when some days I didn't even like the people I worked with? Burnout made sense to me, but I wondered how my heart would handle all the heartbreak.

That's when I came across the work of Charles Figley, who coined the term "compassion fatigue" to further explain burnout specific to those of us in helping professions, describing it as "the cost to caring" for others' emotional pain.[4] I felt a sense of acknowledgment that I was indeed like others who are passionate about work with kids and families but who sometimes feel like they just couldn't care anymore.

It was Gabor Maté's work that finally made it all make sense.[5] He was adamantly against the idea of compassion fatigue. His research reveals that we don't get tired or fatigued with what we are wired to do—connect and care for others. We don't get tired of setting a kid on the right track or hearing a parent say, "Thank you for loving my boy." We get tired when we forget how much we matter, when others don't or aren't able to acknowledge us. Now, I've rarely met a teacher who got into this business for the accolades. I'm talking more about being seen and understood by our partners, our teams, and, sometimes, the families we serve. That, friends, is what keeps us going. On the heels of a global pandemic, everyone is tired. Everyone needs acknowledgment.

Let me tell you a story: It was the day after RELIT! 2020, an annual conference I host, where we virtually gathered three thousand educators and encouraged them to #BringYourBrave. It was magic. I'd made a promise to myself that if (1) the event actually went and stayed live; (2) I managed not to horrifically embarrass myself; and (3) I didn't have to spend multiple hours putting out fires, then I would—officially—consider the event a win. Update: It was a win! No fires, no blunders, just moments of pure awe and inspiration, watching people rise, give, serve, acknowledge, love. But not forty-eight hours later, there I sat, hating people. And life. And wondering why more people don't listen to Mr. Rogers. He had it right forty-six years ago. And how, in all my privilege, do I even have the right to feel this way? I spent some time trying to snap out of it and practice some damn gratitude. Fuck you, gratitude. Not today.

So, let's just take a hot second here and unpack this, because I know I'm not alone. If it's not you or one of your colleagues in this space this moment, I can promise it will be someday. You cannot do hard heart-work and not get tired. Especially when we're more comfortable giving away love and compassion than receiving it.

We don't talk about the cost of this work on helping professionals nearly enough. We don't give teachers enough permission to be tired. To not like kids sometimes. To wonder if on the days they don't feel like Mary Poppins or Mr. Rogers, they're still good teachers. If they've chosen the right profession. If their passion will ever return.

Here's what I know: when you do good work, you will have bad days. Prepare to repair your own heart in this business. But even if you do all the prep in the world, it won't ward off the pain of a bad day. The intent is not to avoid the broken-hearted moments and the criticism and play small, but instead to know that bravery will require you to step in with your whole heart, especially when you can't predict the outcome. If you're going to give your heart away, it's going to get broken.

Acknowledging that we're not alone in the mess helps. You have to sink in before you come up. The key is to not get stuck in the pit of despair for too long, but you never want to skip this part. And sometimes it takes a while to get down there.

The question, of course, is "Then what?" What if you've been spinning in this despair pit for days, months, years? What if you're expected to just suck it up? If you were helping anyone else out of the pit, you'd know what to say. It's just that we forget when it comes time to do it for ourselves. Before we go about fixing it, we have to normalize that holy work is hard work; it's why so many people can't sustain it. If we start by acknowledging that burnout is real and we need to help ourselves first, then we can make a difference.

You will not survive this well if you're disconnected or safely protected behind a wall of avoidance. You may be able to numb some of the pain, but you'll also numb the joy, which is potentially more harmful to you and your loved ones. Believe me, if there's anyone who deserves a little joy around here, it's you. Here are a few things we want you to think about as you reconnect with the people you love, lead, and teach—and, most importantly, with yourself.

Some Strategies
(Because We Know You Love Strategies)

Get out your highlighters. This is where you'll need them the most. In their groundbreaking book *Burnout: The Secret to Unlocking the Stress Cycle,* the Nagoski sisters tell us that exhaustion happens when we get stuck in the emotion: "Just because you've dealt with the stressor, it doesn't mean you've dealt with the stress."[6] In other words, if we do not have people to stay connected to when this job gets too hard, we will get stuck. We will question our work and our worth. So how do we move through that emotional quicksand?

Reconnection

I want to be clear that this connection thing is never, ever over. You will always be in a state of reconnecting. Reconnecting to your why, your health, your hopes, your babies, and your partner is crucial. With whom or what do you want to reconnect? Get them in your head right now. If it's your best friend, call them. If it's a thing like drinking (enough damn) water, make a note of it and do it a little more often. The data are clear: reconnecting with your body via physical exercise—any way you want to move it—is the hands-down best way to survive the hard things.[7] And, as with the kids and families we serve, when we need it most, it's hardest to do. Go ahead and have big dreams about running half marathons or drinking kale smoothies every morning, but start small. In this moment, just a five-minute treadmill break, a stand-up-and-stretch-right-now break is all you need.

You know what else is a foolproof strategy? Reconnecting to your breath. Crazy, but true. In for five, out for ten. Do it with me. You know how good you feel after you take a pause and a few deep breaths. Put 'er on repeat, you saucy chicken.

Rest

When things slow down for me, I start to question everything. I start to feel guilty for indulging in peace and quiet. Sound familiar? As a psychologist, one of the questions on a basic assessment of mental well-being is, "How's your sleep?" I promise you, if you're not getting enough sound sleep, it's the gateway to emotional disaster. Case in point: recall what a toddler looks like when they miss their nap. You're no different. Rest doesn't have to just be sleeping, however. It can also be laughing, eating good food, reading a book. (Look at you, resting right now, you badass!) Just notice, dear one, how much time you're giving to your recharge moments. Find your version of rest wherever and however you can. And remember, it's an average. Some days it will be impossible. And that's OK.

Joy

Joy and happiness are two different things. Remember when we talked about meaning at the beginning of all this? Happiness is generally much more available when you know why you're on this planet. Although you have moments of happiness, the quest to be continually happy isn't reasonable or attainable. But joy, she's a special breed. My friend, Jess Janzen, wrote a necessary little book called *Bring the Joy* after her son Lewiston died of a genetic condition when he was just 179 days old.[8] From her I've learned that even in your darkest moments, joy remains a choice. You will and should sink into exhaustion, pain, and overwhelm. But you also deserve to sink into joy. Seek, and you will find it. Belly laugh with your babies. Dance in your kitchen. Enjoy a dozen funny memes. Laugh till you cry. You need a little more oxytocin in your life. And joy is there, at the ready.

Gratitude

This gratitude thing is important, and it's a practice, just like your golf swing or mindfulness. If we don't practice, we get rusty and, eventually, seize up. I can almost promise you're not very good at it. We are so much better at finding all the things that aren't going well. Look around and notice just a few of the things or people you're thankful for. Then answer me this: Why are they lucky to have you? What do you bring to this family? This team? These babies? Don't just skim over these questions, dammit—answer each one of them. If you can't come up with a single thing, ask your people. They will tell you. Because you're amazing. And we, for two, are so glad you're here.

I'm now going to turn it over to Laurie to highlight the wisdom in the stories you shared with us.

The Chapter That Had to Be Written

We noticed something very interesting when we reviewed the stories teachers sent us. One hundred seventy were about relationships, ninety-five were about trauma, and only seven were about repair.

We need to share the fuck-ups, too. When you do good work, you'll have bad days. But it's how we overcome them that truly matters. You'll notice this chapter is not about how to make kids apologize. This is not their work. It's ours.

Am I Worth It?

Learning to apologize takes practice being vulnerable and courageous enough to right a wrong. It takes someone modeling it for you. I never learned this skill. It wasn't something I was exposed to. But the more we get apologies, the more we can give them. Conflict is inevitable; the ability to repair is critical. Repair is just one more way to answer the all-important question, "Am I worth it?"

Normalize Apologizing

Healing takes time, community, and connection. If you're someone who, like me, struggles with apologies, Stephanie's story might help you, too.

Stephanie's Story

During a volleyball practice in grade ten, our coach was particularly frustrated with the team. When I was confused about what I was supposed to do during a drill, he called me out in front of the whole team. He stopped the drill, then made me continue while my teammates critiqued what I was doing wrong. It was humiliating.

After practice, I ran to the bathroom and cried, then packed up my belongings and walked home. I felt shame, sadness, and frustration. A short time later, the phone rang. It was my coach calling to apologize. When I heard his apology, it felt odd. I couldn't remember an adult ever apologizing to me. I spent the rest of the night (and apparently many years after) reflecting on this experience. As mad as I was, I appreciated that he owned up to his mistake and that he actually did something to fix our relationship. I never forgot that exchange. Or that coach.

Forgiveness

So much of the work we do centers around forgiving ourselves for past mistakes and releasing guilt. I don't always get this right. It just isn't humanly possible to make this many decisions in one day and please everyone, including myself, at all times. I know when I have made a mistake, and I know that even if I repair it with that colleague or student, the harder part comes with forgiving myself.

Tiffany's Story

It was my second year of teaching. One child in my class had been flipping his lid for a solid hour. He crawled underneath a bookshelf with the assignment he'd worked on for months. He looked me dead in the eye, poised to rip it to pieces. I yelled: "STOP IT! DON'T YOU DARE!" loud enough to shake the room. All of my students' eyes were on me. In my limited experience as a very young teacher, I had no strategies for a follow-up. I was exhausted from the previous hour's negotiations and overcome by my own frustration with what he was about to do. His response to my yelling was to freeze. He didn't rip up the assignment, but what happened next was so much worse. He put his assignment down, buried his head in his knees, and started to cry. Looking back on this moment now it breaks my heart. If I could go back, I would not have taken his actions so personally. I would have responded with empathy to the frustration he must have been feeling. I loved that kid, and I still think about him. I wish I could go back and redo that moment.

Take some time to reflect on how you can move forward with forgiving yourself for the mistakes you've made. We've all been there. And we all will be there again. I often think of this David Jeremiah quote when I find myself in Tiffany's shoes: "Forgiveness prompted by love is the only way to repair the devastation that so often mars our relationships."[9]

Reconnection

When I'm filled up, many of the strategies we've talked about in this book come easily. But, when I'm not, they seem impossible to attain. I know the best thing I can do for myself in those moments is to reconnect, whether it's with my mom, an old friend, my own little family, or myself. Here are a few reconnection strategies I've been taught along the way.

Breaking or Building?

Are you breaking or building attachment? That's it. Challenge yourself to get into the habit of asking yourself, with every interaction, "Am I breaking this connection right now or building it?"

The strategy fits beautifully with this quote from Deborah MacNamara: "When a child is attached to their teacher, they are inclined to follow them, listen, want to be the same as, talk like, be good for, inclined to agree with, take direction from, be open to influence from, and seek to measure up. The characteristics that make kids easy to teach are the result of healthy attachment—not teaching style, technology, curriculum, or classroom."[10]

I ask myself this question dozens of times a day. In fact, I have hearts posted around the room with the words "breaking or building" as a visual reminder of just how important it is. Some of my best "builders" involve adding or enhancing voice and choice in our classroom community. Democratizing so students get a say in where we go and how we get there and allowing them to be the leaders and experts in our room often lead them to saying things like, "Thank you for letting us vote. It made my heart feel happy to be here." Building: check.

Reflection

Every week, I ask myself these four reflection questions:

1. What did I learn this week?

2. Am I on track for our learners to feel the way I want when they leave my classroom in June?
3. Did I treat every learner as I would want my own kids to be treated? Is there anything I need to repair?
4. If today was your last day in the classroom, would you be proud of how you ended it?

Honest reflection helps me find gratitude in our classroom community, to set goals for the upcoming week, and to reconnect with where we're going. While the questions might look different for you, what's relevant is the process of reflecting and forgiving. Most important, this process allows me to rest.

Rest

Rest makes us healthier, happier teachers. It allows us to renew and show up the best we can. Practice loving a no-work day. Let yourself stay in those PJs, drink copious amounts of coffee, and binge Netflix. But also remember that that's not the only kind of rest that's beneficial. You have to find ways to incorporate rest into every day.

Boundaries around the Awfulizers

Part of rest involves boundaries. Rest from expectations, my own and others'. And my favorite boundary is what I like to call "minimizing exposure."

I minimize my exposure to the joy-suckers of the world. The "awfulizers," as Jimmy Casas calls them.[11] The ones who say shit like, "But we've always done it this way," or "Don't get your hopes up," or the worst one, "It's easy for you because . . . " Gross.

With these pleasant little muffins, I like to be polite and present when it's necessary to be around them, but I do what it takes to minimize my exposure to them, whether on social media or in my own personal universe. It's key to my rest. By minimizing my exposure, I save myself from the subsequent time-waster of having conversations with them in my head (what I could or should have said). I don't need to reflect on whether they had a point. I don't need to plant seeds of doubt in my own mind. I can simply rest.

My Four Ws

When I feel tired, I often turn to my mom for guidance. With my husband working out of town, three kids, and a full-time job, she's my go-to when I feel like I just can't take one more step. During these conversations, she asks, "What is one thing you can take off the to-do list?"

This inspired me to create another series of reflection questions I ask when I feel like rest is impossible (another classic sign of burnout). These four Ws help me find rest when I need it the most.

- WHO can help me with the problems I'm facing right now?
- WHAT can be taken off the to-do list? Not checked off, *taken* off or delegated.
- WHEN will I take time to purposely rest today?
- WHERE will I rest?

Conserve your energy for what matters. You can offer this world so much more when you allow yourself to rest.

Joy

When my ratio of creating to consuming the world around me starts to get skewed, I go off course. I feel more tired, irritable, and anxious. That's when I know I have consumed too much and need to go into creation mode. And my favorite thing to create? Joy.

I love finding opportunities to create joy. It's literally in my lesson plans. If I wake up in the morning dreading what I've planned for the day, it will indeed suck. Adding the line, "Where will you find and create joy today?" into my plans helps me set the tone and my intention for the day.

When I was ready to quit teaching years ago, I knew I had to bring joy back into what I was doing. Inspired by my Ellen experience, #KindnessCapes were born. Every month, I planned a kindness mission for our kids: Planning and delivering treats to the high school students during exam week. Hiding student-made bookmarks in our library's books. Heading downtown armed with sidewalk chalk to leave messages of hope and inspiration.

At the time, I only looked forward to those days. I would put them on my calendar and try to focus on the love and joy we would feel no matter how shitty the other days felt. Needless to say, after a few months, things had changed. Kindness missions became a daily occurrence, a mindset and culture our class was built on. They're still my favorite days in our classroom.

Kindness may not be your passion—that's OK! Maybe yours is an art project you love, a game of dodgeball, or exploring nature with photography. Find your way to plan for joy.

Gratitude

Gratitude is another situation in which the more you give it, the more you get it. We need to not just tell kids we're grateful for them (which is a great start, by the way), we also need to show them.

As I walk to my car each night, I name all the students I'm grateful for. The last three names go on a note I tuck into my pocket for the next day. Chances are, if I named them last, we probably need a connection boost. Having the note in my pocket reminds me to seek those three out to tell them how grateful I am for them and why.

When a staff member comes to visit or brings us back from a class they've taught, instead of a monotonous, whole-class "Thank you," we share why we're grateful for them. We have "We are grateful for ___" days throughout the year. We designate one child or staff member as the day's honoree, then decorate a giant heart with everything they mean to us and present it to them as a special keepsake. We pass around a gratitude rock with the words "thank you" on it and share what we are most grateful for that day. From our Kindergarten Kindness Kart filled with snacks and drinks for our staff to notes stuck to lockers for kids to find, practicing gratitude brings us together.

Meaghan's Story

I'm an English teacher. And English 30-2, in my personal opinion, calls for *Tuesdays with Morrie*, a memoir by Mitch Albom about the dynamics of a teacher–student relationship and the life lessons shared each Tuesday as Morrie Schwartz is slowly taken by ALS. It resonates so deeply with me when a teacher affects a student to their core, earning their respect and love just for being one's true self and helping them navigate life. It's the influence every educator one day hopes to have.

One year, I didn't feel I was doing the book (or my kids, for that matter) the justice it deserved. I felt pulled in a million directions. I was exhausted and feared my students wouldn't understand what made this book so meaningful to me, which, as their teacher, was devastating.

Then, one random Tuesday, I found a small package on my desk. Roughly wrapped and taped, no card. I opened it. Inside was a copy of *Long Time Running*, a documentary about the Tragically Hip. They were one of my favorite bands, a Canadian staple, and someone had found a copy of this DVD just for me. It was used, which means it was loved by another fan, and I was thankful for the sweet mystery gift.

Then, peeking from the inside flap, I saw a torn scrap of paper. A fragment that could have easily been lost. On it was my most precious teacher treasure to date:

"Thanks for being my Morrie. ~ Cam"

Reconnect, rest, practice joy, and show gratitude. And know this: you are so many somebodies' Morrie.

Wrapping Up and Moving On

Here's the deal: fixing is often so different from repairing. Quick fixes are usually laden with suggestions and strategies. But repair takes work. It often requires rebuilding, sometimes breaking it down even further so you can rebuild it even stronger. We can repair so much easier if we're not burned out. Surround yourself with people who help you feel acknowledged, so you can continue to teach and be better for it. Here's our three, two, one, ready for when you need it.

Three things to try

- Think about your current students and imagine their respective experiences with apology and repair. If warranted, see how they respond to an apology.
- Set a timer on your phone or your watch to go off every hour during the school day. When it does, breathe, slowly and deeply, and remind yourself that you are changing lives.
- Notice one new thing about someone in your house, like how their hands rest on the table or how they wear their hair. If you live alone, choose a neighbor, pet, friend, or even yourself. Just notice.

Two quotes to consider

"Apologizing doesn't always mean that you're wrong and the other person is right. It just means that you value your relationship more than your ego." —Mark Matthews

"Burnout is what happens when you avoid being human for too long." —Michael Gungor

One question to answer

- Why are they lucky to have you? It's a tough one to answer, and it will change with the seasons. So, ask it of yourself and your team often.

Conclusion

An educator and a psychologist walk into a bar. One doesn't drink. (You guess which one.) Just kidding: that educator and that psychologist met over their passion for kids and those who hold them and, after two years of collaboration, a book for teachers was born. This is the final scene, our closing act. When we thought about what we wanted to leave you with, here's what we came up with—we don't want to leave. We feel so connected and indebted to you for reading these words, for shaping developing minds and holding tender hearts, for being (hopefully) a part of this community of amazing teachers who have come together.

To us, teachers are heroes. Sure, there are those who don't step up, for whatever reason, but most teachers we've met are so incredibly woven into every community they teach in. Bravery is part of being a hero. And we love the word "brave." Really love it. It's not brave if you know how it's going to end. If there's no risk or vulnerability involved, courage isn't required. As a teacher, choosing to step in with your whole heart, alongside other people's most precious commodity—their children—you have to be brave. Every day. You cannot predict the mix of emotions, hormones, joys, and pains. It's so rarely about lesson plans or the literacy or the numeracy. The bravest among you make the biggest difference. You leave the most significant legacy through connecting, and reconnecting, with your students, your players, your colleagues.

We want to leave you with the knowledge that your leadership in your space, whatever that looks like, is absolutely critical. Abby Wambach reminds us about the importance of "leading from the bench."[1] We can all be leaders and cheerleaders at any given moment. Our biggest job is to just step up. Although every educational building has a hierarchical leadership structure, know that you have the potential to be a leader, too.

This book, sweet teachers, is all about the connection. The power that comes with investing in fears and feelings. We see you. We know how hard you try. Just how much you've given when no one was watching. As you step back into classrooms, lecture halls, bus lanes, or noisy hallways in the days, weeks, and years that lie ahead, our biggest hope is that you will remember this: You are being written into so many chapters at this very moment. What people will remember most about you, your legacy, will have so much more to do with a felt sense than it ever will with words or numbers. Your only job, dear teacher, is to shine that incredible light that brought you into this profession in the first place. We are so grateful to you for reading these words but, more importantly, for serving our children. Whatever you got on any given day is (more than) enough. And when it gets dim or the path gets too rough, we hope you will land back here, in these pages, or in the platforms where we will be waiting to remind you of your power, your promise, and your contribution to this planet—all because you are a teacher. xo

Endnotes

Introduction

1   Maetche, S. (2015, March 5). Local teacher pays it forward after Ellen show appearance. *Lacombe Express*. Retrieved from lacombeexpress .com/news/local-teacher-pays-it-forward-after-ellen-show -appearance/

2   Find more about James Clear at jamesclear.com.

Chapter 1

1   Find more about Shawn Achor at shawnachor.com.

2   Vallerand, R. J., Blanchard, C., Mageau, G. A., Koestner, R., Ratelle, C., Léonard, M., Gagné, M., & Marsolais, J. (2003). Les passions de l'âme: On obsessive and harmonious passion. *Journal of Personality and Social Psychology, 85*(4), 756–767. doi. org/10.1037/0022-3514.85.4.756

3   Vallerand, R. J. (2008). On the psychology of passion: In search of what makes people's lives most worth living. *Canadian Psychology/ Psychologie canadienne, 49*(1), 1–13. doi.org/10.1037/0708-5591.49 .1.1

4   LeShure, E. (2019, March 5). *We are literally in two realities at the same time.* A Mindful Emergence. amindfulemergence.com/ what-is-dual-awareness/

5   Duval, T. S., Silvia, P. J., & Lalwani, N. (2012). *Self-awareness and causal attribution: A dual systems theory.* Springer Science & Business Media.

6   Shipp, J. *The power of one caring adult.* joshshipp.com/one-caring -adult

Chapter 2

1   Bronfenbrenner, U. (1991). What do families do? *Institute for American Values*, Winter / Spring, 2

2   Brendto, L. K. (2006). The vision of Urie Bronfenbrenner: Adults who are crazy about kids. *Reclaiming Children and Youth, 15*(3), 162–166. Retrieved from cyc-net.org/cyc-online/cyconline-nov2010-brendtro .html

3   Shanker, S. (2017). *Self-reg: How to help your child (and you) break the stress cycle and successfully engage with life*. Penguin Books.

4   Siegel, D. (2012, February 8). *"Flipping your lid": A scientific explanation*. Dalai Lama Center for Peace and Education. youtu.be/G0T_2NNoC68

5   Momentous Institute. (2019, April 7). *Upstairs and downstairs brain*. momentousinstitute.org/blog/upstairs-and-downstairs-brain

6   Butler, D. B., Schnellert, L., & Cartier, S. C. (2013). Layers of self- and co-regulation: Teachers working collaboratively to support adolescents' self-regulated learning through reading. *Education Research International, 2013*, 1–19. dx.doi.org/10.1155/2013/845694

7   Find more information at circleofsecurityinternational.com.

8   Hoffman, K., Cooper, G., Powell, B., Siegle, D. J., & Benton, C. M. (2017). *Raising a secure child: How Circle of Security parenting can help you nurture your child's attachment, emotional resilience, and freedom to explore*. Guilford Press.

9   Casas, J. (2017). *Culturize: Every student. Every day. Whatever it takes*. Dave Burgess Consulting, Inc.

10   Greene, R. (2014). *The explosive child: A new approach for understanding and parenting easily* (5th ed.). Harper Paperbacks.

11   Find more about A.J. Juliani at ajjuliani.com.

12   Cook, C. R., et al. (2018). Positive greetings at the door: Evaluation of a low-cost, high-yield proactive classroom management strategy. *Journal of Positive Behaviour Interventions, 20*(3). doi.org/10.1177/1098300717753831

13   Nelson, C. B. (2015, November 1). Latest research says praising employees boosts productivity after all. *Forbes*. Retrieved from forbes.com/sites/christophernelson/2015/11/01/latest-research -says-praising-employees-boosts-productivity-after-all/?sh =585cdd595f80

Chapter 3

1   Perry, B. D., & Winfrey, O. (2021). *What happened to you? Conversations on trauma, resilience, and healing*. Flatiron Books.

2   Find more about Jesse Lipscombe at talentbureau.com/speaker/jesse-lipscombe.

3   American Psychiatric Association. (2013). *Diagnostic and statistical manual of mental disorders* (5th ed.). doi.org/10.1176/appi.books .9780890425596

4   Muris, P., & Ollendick, T. H. (2005). The role of temperament in the etiology of child psychopathology. *Clinical Child and Family Psychology Review, 8*(4), 271–289. doi.org/10.1007/s10567-005-8809-y

5   Saad, L. (2020). *Me and white supremacy: How to recognise your privilege, combat racism and change the world.* Quercus.

6   Yingst T. E. (2011). Cultural bias. In: Goldstein S., & Naglieri J. A. (Eds.), *Encyclopedia of Child Behavior and Development.* Springer. (pp. 233–256). doi.org/10.1007/978-0-387-79061-9_749

7   Lindgren, K. P., Kaysen, D., Werntz, A. J., Gasser, M. L., & Teachman, B. A. (2013). Wounds that can't be seen: Implicit trauma associations predict posttraumatic stress disorder symptoms. *Journal of Behavior Therapy and Experimental Psychiatry, 44*(4), 368–375. doi.org/10.1016/j.jbtep.2013.03.003

8   O'Brien, N., & Tabb, L. (2020). *Unpack your impact: How two primary teachers ditched problematic lessons and built a culture-centered curriculum.* Dave Burgess Consulting, Inc.

9   Hierck. T. (2016). *Seven keys to a positive learning environment in your classroom.* Solution Tree. (p. 65)

Chapter 4

1   Matheson, K., Foster, M. D., Bombay, A., McQuaid, R. J., & Anisman, H. (2019). Traumatic experiences, perceived discrimination, and psychological distress among members of various socially marginalized groups. *Frontiers in Psychology, 10*, 1–16. doi.org/10.3389/fpsyg.2019.00416

2   Van der Kolk, B. (2002). Trauma and memory. *Psychiatry and Clinical Neurosciences, 52*(51). doi.org/10.1046/j.1440-1819.1998.0520s5S97.x

3   Dumbo, E. A., & Sabatino, C. A. (2019). *Creating trauma-informed schools: A guide for school social workers and educators.* Oxford Scholarship Online. doi:10.1093/oso/9780190873806.003.0003

4   Felitti, V. J., et al. (1998). Relationship of childhood abuse and household dysfunction to many of the leading causes of death in adults. *American Journal of Preventive Medicine, 14*(4), 245–258. doi.org/10.1016/S0749-3797(98)00017-8

5   Balas, E. A., & Boren, S.A. (2000). Managing clinical knowledge for health care improvement. *Yearbook of Medical Informatics, 1*, 65–70. PMID: 27699347

6   Heneghan, C., Goldacre, B., & Mahtani, K. R. (2017). Why clinical trial outcomes fail to translate into benefits for patients. *BMC Trials, 18*(122). doi.org/10.1186/s13063-017-1870-2

7   Thompson, S. (2014). *Encyclopedia of diversity and social justice.* Rowman & Littlefield Publishers.

8   Delgado, R., & Stefancic, J. (2017). *Critical race theory: An introduction.* NYU Press.

9   Edmondson, L. (1976). Trans-Atlantic slavery and the internationalization of race. *Caribbean Quarterly, Essays on Slavery, 22*(2/3), 5–25

10 Olusoga, D. (2015, September 8). The roots of European racism lie in the slave trade, colonialism—and Edward Long. *The Guardian.* theguardian.com/commentisfree/2015/sep/08/european-racism-africa-slavery

11 Jenkins, J. P. (2016, November 30). White supremacy. *Encyclopedia Britannica*. britannica.com/topic/white-supremacy

12 Union of International Associations. (2020, June 16). White supremacy. *The Encyclopedia of World Problems and Human Potential.* encyclopedia.uia.org/en/problem/136157

13 Rotz, S. (2017). "They took our beads, it was a fair trade, get over it": Settler colonial logics, racial hierarchies and material dominance in Canadian agriculture. *Geoforum, 82,* 158–169. doi.org/10.1016/j.geoforum.2017.04.010

14 Miller, J. R. (2010; updated 2021). Residential schools in Canada. *The Canadian Encyclopedia.* thecanadianencyclopedia.ca/en/article/residential-schools

15 Truth and Reconciliation Commission of Canada. (n.d.). Residential school locations. trc.ca/about-us/residential-school.html

16 National Centre for Truth and Reconciliation (2015). Final report and recommendations. nctr.ca/reports.php

17 Trembath, T., & Rieger, S. (2021, May 31). More than 800 residential school students died in Alberta—advocates say its time to find their graves. *CBC News.* Retrieved from: cbc.ca/news/canada/calgary/residential-school-graves-alberta-1.6046329

18 Sinclair, N., & Dainard, S. (2016; updated 2020). Sixties scoop. *The Canadian Encyclopedia.* thecanadianencyclopedia.ca/en/article/sixties-scoop

19 Manne, R. (2017). *Down girl: The logic of misogyny.* Oxford University Press.

20 First Nations Child and Family Services. (2020). Reducing the number of Indigenous children in care. sac-isc.gc.ca/eng/1541187352297/1541187392851

21 To learn more about what is being done to change these numbers and read An Act respecting First Nations, Inuit and Métis children, youth and families (S.C. 2019, c. 24), visit laws.justice.gc.ca/eng/acts/F-11.73/index.html.

22 Matz, D., Vogel, E.B., Mattar, S., & Montenegro, H. (2015). Interrupting intergenerational trauma: Children of Holocaust survivors and the Third Reich. *Journal of Phenomenological Psychology, 46*(2), 185–205

23 Sangalang, C. C., & Vang, C. (2017). Intergenerational trauma in refugee families. *Journal of Immigrant and Minority Health, 19*(3), 745–754

24 Alberta Children and Family Services. (2020). *Child intervention information and statistics summary: 2020/21 first quarter (June) update.* open.alberta.ca/dataset/de167286-500d-4cf8-bf01-0d08224eeadc/resource/135927f4-e9c0-4181-a148-b2f199f0666a/download/cs-child-intervention-information-statistics-summary-2020-2021-q1.pdf

25 Kumar, M. B., & Tjepkema, M. (2019, June 28). *Suicide among First Nations people, Métis and Inuit (2011–2016): Findings from the 2011 Canadian Census Health and Environment Cohort (CanCHEC).* Statistics Canada. www150.statcan.gc.ca/n1/pub/99-011-x/99-011-x2019001-eng.htm.

26 Sherman, J., Rasmussen, C., & Wikman, E. (2006). ADHD characteristics in Canadian Aboriginal children. *Journal of Attention Disorders, 9*(4), 642–647. doi.org/10.1177/1087054705284246

27 McMahon, T. (2014, August 22). Why fixing First Nations education remains so far out of reach: Aboriginal youth face a fate that should horrify Canadians and there's an obvious fix. *Maclean's.* macleans.ca/news/canada/why-fixing-first-nations-education-remains-so-far-out-of-reach/

28 Gordon, C., & White, J. P. (2014). Indigenous educational attainment in Canada. *International Indigenous Policy Journal, 5*(3). doi.org/10.18584/iipj.2014.5.3.6

29 University of Michigan. (n.d.). *An instructor's guide to understanding privilege.* sites.lsa.umich.edu/inclusive-teaching/an-instructors-guide-to-understanding-privilege/

30 Oluo, I. (2019). *So you want to talk about race.* Seal Press.

31 Crenshaw, K. (1993). Mapping the margins: Intersectionality, identity politics, and violence against women of color. *Stanford Law Review, 43*(6), 1241–1299. doi.org/10.2307/1229039

32 Tabb, L., & O'Brien, N. (2020). *A white families' guide to talking about racism.* laneshatabb.com/home/store28348178-company-site/A-White-Families-Guide-to-Talking-About-Racism-p205029857

33 Mueller, J., & Nickel, J. (Eds.). (2019). *Globalization and diversity: What does it mean for teacher education in Canada?* Canadian Association for Teacher Education. cate-acfe.ca/wp-content/uploads/2019/11/Final-Working-Conference-Book-Halifax-2017.pdf

34 Ryan, J., Pollock, K., & Antonelli, F. (2009). Teacher diversity in Canada: Leaky pipelines, bottlenecks, and glass ceilings. *Canadian Journal of Education, 32*(3), 591–617

35 Kubota, J., Banaji, M.R., & Phelps, E.A. (2012). The neuroscience of race. *Nature Neuroscience, 15*, 940–948.

36 Brown, B. (2017). *Rising strong: How the ability to reset transforms the way we live, love, parent, and lead.* Random House.

37 Hanson, R. F., & Lang, J. (2016). Critical look at trauma-informed care among agencies and systems serving maltreated youth and their families. *Child Maltreatment, 21*(2), 95–100. doi.org/10.1177/1077559516635274

38 Maynard, B. R., Farina, A., Dell, N. A., & Kelly, M. S. (2019). Effects of trauma-informed approaches in schools: A systematic review. *Campbell Systematic Reviews, 15*(1–2). doi.org/10.1002/cl2.1018

39 For more information, see carringtonnetwork.com.

40 Ellis, S., & Tod, J. (2018). *Behaviour for learning: Promoting positive relationships in the classroom.* Routledge.

41 Perfect, M. M, Turley, M. R., Carlson, J. S., Yohanna, J., & Pfenninger-Saint Gilles, M. (2016). School-related outcomes of traumatic event exposure and traumatic stress symptoms in students: A systematic review of research from 1990 to 2015. *School Mental Health, 8*(1), 7–43. doi.org/10.1007/s12310-016-9175-2

42 Nordoff, K. (2019). *Exploring equity issues: Introduction to trauma-informed classrooms: inclusive learning strategies for educators.* Center for Education Equity. maec.org/wp-content/uploads/2019/06/Exploring-Equity-Trauma-Informed-Classrooms-Primer.pdf

43 Allen, R., Jerrim, J., & Sims, S. (2020). *How did the early stages of the COVID-19 pandemic affect teacher wellbeing?* CEPEO Working Paper

No. 20-15, Centre for Education Policy and Equalising Opportunities, UCL. EconPapers.repec.org/RePEc:ucl:cepeow:20-15.

44 World Health Organization, *Constitution*, who.int/about/governance/constitution

45 Narayan, A. J., Rivera, L. M., Bernstein, R. E., Harris, W. W., & Lieberman A. F. (2018). Positive childhood experiences predict less psychopathology and stress in pregnant women with childhood adversity: A pilot study of the Benevolent Childhood Experiences (BCEs) Scale. *Child Abuse & Neglect, 78,* 19–30. doi.org/10.1016/j .chiabu.2017.09.022

46 Bethell, C., Jones, J., Gombojav, N., Linkenbach, J., & Sege, R. (2019). Positive childhood experiences and adult mental and relational health in a statewide sample: Associations across adverse childhood experiences levels. *JAMA Pediatrics, 173*(11). doi.org:10.1001/jamapediatrics.2019.3007

47 Ross, N., Gilbert, R., Torres, S., Dugas, K., Jefferies, P., McDonald, S., Savage, S., & Ungar, M. (2020). Adverse childhood experiences: Assessing the impact on physical and psychosocial health in adulthood and the mitigating role of resilience. *Child Abuse & Neglect, 103.* doi.org/10.1016/j.chiabu.2020.104440

48 Narayan, A. J., et al. (2018). Positive childhood experiences predict less psychopathology and stress in pregnant women with childhood adversity: A pilot study of the Benevolent Childhood Experiences (BCEs) Scale. *Child Abuse & Neglect, 78,* 19–30. doi.org/10.1016/j .chiabu.2017.09.022

49 van der Kolk, B. (2014). *The body keeps the score: Brain, mind, and body in the healing of trauma.* Viking Press.

50 Parker, J. (2019, September 2). *Hope is in the struggle.* Medium. joshparker1422.medium.com/hope-is-in-the-struggle-2d57a211558e

51 Sporleder, J., & Forbes, H. T . (2016). *The trauma-informed school: A step-by-step implementation guide for administrators and school personnel.* Beyond Consequences Institute Inc.

52 Summersault, A. (2020, October 26). *The savior complex: An honest look at your toxic codependence.* Medium. medium.com/be-unique/the-savior-complex-an-honest-look-at-your-toxic-codependence -e6295e80e2ef

53 Find more about Dr. Sonia Lupien at theroyal.ca/research/biography/dr-sonia-lupien.

54   Centre for Studies on Human Stress, *Recipe for stress*, humanstress.
     ca/stress/understand-your-stress/sources-of-stress

55   Brown, B. (2015). *Rising strong.* Random House.

Chapter 5

1   Koblenz, J. (2016). Growing from grief: Qualitative experiences of
     parental loss. OMEGA –*Journal of Death and Dying, 73*(3). doi.org/10
     .1177/0030222815576123

2   Apelian, E., & Nesteruk, O. (2017). Reflections of young adults on
     the loss of a parent in adolescence. *International Journal of Child,
     Youth and Family Studies, 8*(3–4), 79–100. dx.doi.org/10.18357/
     ijcyfs83/4201718002

3   Allen, J. (n.d.). *Death ed.: Grief and loss education.* deathed.ca

4   Wolfet, A.D. (2016, November 16). *Exploring your feelings of loss.*
     Center for Loss & Life Transition. centerforloss.com/2016/11/
     exploring-feelings-loss/

5   Wolfelt, A. D. (2001). *Healing your grieving heart.* Companion Press.

6   Wolfelt, A.D. (n.d.). *The six needs of mourning.* Center for Loss & Life
     Transition. centerforloss.com/grief/six-needs-mourning

7   Allen, J. G., & Haccoun, D. M. (1976). Sex differences in emotionality:
     A multidimensional approach. *Human Relations 29*, 711–722

8   Chaplin, T. M., Cole, P. M., & Zahn-Waxler, C. (2005). Parental
     socialization of emotion expression: Gender differences
     and relations to child adjustment. *Emotion, 5*, 80–88.
     doi:10.1037/1528–3542.5.1.80

9   Chaplin T. M. (2015). Gender and emotion expression: A
     developmental contextual perspective. *Emotion Review, 7*(1), 14–21.
     doi.org/10.1177/1754073914544408

10   Reynolds, C., White, R., Brayman, C., & Moore, S. (2008). Women
     and secondary school principal rotation/succession: A study of the
     beliefs of decision makers in four provinces. *Canadian Journal of
     Education, 31*(1), 32–54

11   Morrison, N. (2018, April 12). White men are still over-represented
     in school leadership. *Forbes.* Retrieved from forbes.
     com/sites/nickmorrison/2018/04/12/white-men-are-stil
     l-over-represented-in-school-leadership/?sh=633c89b06019

12   Young, L., Levin, B., & Wallin, D. (2014). *Understanding Canadian
     schools: An introduction to educational administration* (5th ed.). home
     .cc.umanitoba.ca/~wallind/understandingcanadianschools5.html

13 Albom, M. (1997). *Tuesdays with Morrie: An old man, a young man, and life's greatest lesson*. Crown Publishing.

14 Papadatou, D., Metallinou, O., Hatzichristou, C., & Pavlidi, L. (2002). Supporting the bereaved child: Teacher's perceptions and experiences in Greece. *Mortality, 7*, 324–339. doi.org/10.1080/1357627021000025478

15 Engarhos, P., Shohoudi, A., Crossman, A., & Talwar, V. (2020). Learning through observing: Effects of modeling truth- and lie-telling on children's honesty. *Developmental Science, 23*(1), e12883–n/a. doi.org/10.1111/desc.12883

16 Renaud, S., Engarhos, P., Schleifer, M., & Talwar, V. (2015). Children's earliest experiences with death: Circumstances, conversations, explanations, and parental satisfaction. *Infant and Child Development, 24*(2), 157–174. doi.org/10.1002/icd.1889

17 van der Kolk, B. (2015). *The body keeps the score: Brain, mind, and body in the healing of trauma*. Penguin Books.

18 Center for Suicide Prevention. (2013). *Indigenous suicide prevention.* suicideinfo.ca/resource/indigenous-suicide-prevention

19 Public Health Agency of Canada. (2016). *Suicide prevention framework.* canada.ca/en/public-health/services/publications/healthy-living/suicide-prevention-framework.html

20 American Psychological Association. (n.d.). *Marriage and divorce.* apa.org/topics/divorce-child-custody

21 Sinha, M. (2014). *Parenting and child support after separation or divorce.* Statistics Canada. www150.statcan.gc.ca/n1/en/pub/89-652-x/89-652-x2014001-eng.pdf?st=6Z5ZzFMN

22 Statistics Canada. (2019). *Family matters: Being common law, married, separated or divorced in Canada.* www150.statcan.gc.ca/n1/daily-quotidien/190501/dq190501b-eng.htm

23 Potter, D. (2010). Psychosocial well-being and the relationship between divorce and children's academic achievement. *Journal of Marriage and Family, 72*(4), 933–946 doi:10.1111/j.1741-3737.2010.00740.x

24 Kaye, S. H. (2008). The impact of divorce on children's academic performance. *Journal of Divorce, 12*(2–3). doi.org/10.1300/J279v12n02_16

25 Pears, K. C., Kim, H. K., Buchanan, R., & Fisher, P. A. (2015). Adverse consequences of school mobility for children in foster care: A prospective longitudinal study. *Child Development, 86*(4), 1210–1226. doi.org/10.1111/cdev.12374

26 Find more about Elisabeth Kübler-Ross at ekrfoundation.org.

27 Kessler, D. (2019). *Finding meaning: The sixth stage of grief.* Scribner.

28 Ibid.

29 Forsythia, S. (2020). *Your grief, your way: a year of practical guidance and comfort after loss.* Zeitgeist Publishing.

Chapter 6

1 Quoted in Surden, E. (1976, January 26). Privacy laws may usher in "defensive DP": Hopper, *Computerworld, 10*(4), 9.

2 Perry, B. L. & Morris, E. W. (2014). Suspending progress: Collateral consequences of exclusionary punishment in public schools. *American Sociological Review, 79,* 1067–1087.

3 Bacher-Hicks, A., Billings, S. B, & Deming, D. J. (2019). *The school to prison pipeline: The long-run impacts of school suspensions on adult crime.* NBER Working Papers 26257, National Bureau of Economic Research. nber.org/system/files/working_papers/w26257/w26257.pdf

4 NAACP. (2005). *Interrupting the school to prison pipe-line.*

5 Cuellar, A. E., & Markowitz, S. (2015). School suspension and the school-to-prison pipeline. *International Review of Law and Economics, 43*(C), 98–106. doi.org/10.1016/j.irle.2015.06.001

6 APA Public Affairs Office. (2006, August 9). Zero tolerance policies are not as effective as thought [press release]. American Psychological Association. apa.org/news/press/releases/2006/08/zero-tolerance

7 Bacher-Hicks, A., Billings, S. B., & Deming, D. J. (2019). *The school to prison pipeline: long-run impacts of school suspensions on adult crime.* NBER Working Papers 26257, National Bureau of Economic Research. nber.org/system/files/working_papers/w26257/w26257.pdf

8 Cole, N. L. (2020, October 21). *Understanding the school-to-prison pipeline.* thoughtco.com/school-to-prison-pipeline-4136170

9 Covey, S. (1989). *The seven habits of highly effective people.* FranklinCovey.

10 Moore, S. (2022). *All for one: Designing individual education plans for inclusive classrooms.* Portage & Main Press.

11 Siegel, D. (2010). *Mindsight: The new science of personal transformation.* Bantam Publishing.

12 Brown, B. (2012). *The power of vulnerability.* Avery Publishing.

13 Texas A&M University. (2005, April 11). Babies use their own names to help learn language. *ScienceDaily.* sciencedaily.com/releases/2005/05/050513230407.htm

14 Bergland, C. (2012, November 29). The neurochemicals of happiness: Seven brain molecules that make you feel great. *Psychology Today.* psychologytoday.com/ca/blog/the-athletes-way/201211/the -neurochemicals-happiness

15 Murphy, M., Janicki-Deverts, D., & Cohen, S. (2018). Receiving a hug is associated with the attenuation of negative mood that occurs on days with interpersonal conflict. *PloS One, 13*(10), e0203522. doi.org/10.1371/journal.pone.0203522

16 Carnegie, D. *Remembering names.* dalecarnegie.com/en/courses/3741

17 Hogan, A. (2017). *Shattering the perfect teacher myth: 6 truths that will help you thrive as an educator.* Dave Burgess Consulting

Chapter 7

1 Lerner, H. (2017). *Why won't you apologize?: Healing big betrayals and everyday hurts.* Gallery Books.

2 Sweet, P. L. (2019). The sociology of gaslighting. *American Sociological Review, 84*(5), 851–875. doi.org/10.1177/0003122419874843

3 Heinemann, L. V., & Heinemann, T. (2017). Burnout research: emergence and scientific investigation of a contested diagnosis. *Sage Journal.* doi.org/1d0o.i.1o1rg7/71/02.1157872/241450812474609 1716597415

4 Figley, C. R., & Ludick, M. (2017). Secondary traumatization and compassion fatigue. In S. N. Gold (Ed.), *APA handbook of trauma psychology: Foundations in knowledge* (pp. 573–593). American Psychological Association. doi.org/10.1037/0000019-029

5 Maté, G. (2005). *Hold on to your kids: Why parents need to matter more than peers.* Vintage Canada.

6 Nagoski, E. & Nagoski, A. (2019). *Burnout: The secret to unlocking the stress cycle.* Random House.

7 Ochentel, O., Humphrey, C., & Pfeifer, K. (2018). Efficacy of exercise therapy in persons with burnout: A systematic review and meta-analysis. *Journal of Sports Science & Medicine, 17*(3), 475–484

8 Janzen, J. (2020). *Bring the joy.* Fedd Books.

9 Jeremiah, D. (2019). *Overcomer: 8 ways to live a life of unstoppable strength, unmovable faith, and unbelievable power.* Thomas Nelson.

10 MacNamara, D. (2016). *Rest, play, grow: Making sense of preschoolers (or anyone who acts like one).* Aona Books.

11 Casas, J. (2017). *Culturize: Every student. Every day. Whatever it takes.* Dave Burgess Consulting, Inc.

Conculsion

1   Wambach, A. (2019). *Wolfpack: How to come together, unleash our power, and change the game.* Celedon Books.

Acknowledgments

An acknowledgment is the power of holding space and recognizing the importance. It is the expression of indebtedness to others. It is never a one-shot deal. In the most powerful ending to a book that we could imagine, we wanted to acknowledge the privilege we have to be on this land, the people we've been blessed with to walk this journey (there are so many), and you—all of you who do this work and have read these words. Thank you. We are forever indebted.

Jody:

The land: I wrote most of these words on Treaty 7 territory, the traditional territories of the Blackfoot Nations, including the Siksika, Piikani, and Kainai Nations, the Tsuut'ina Nation and Stoney Nakoda First Nations. I am humbled, honored, and privileged to raise our babies on this sacred ground and acknowledge the many First Nations, Métis, and Inuit peoples whose footsteps marked these lands for centuries. My role in reconciliation has only just begun and will never end.

And to all my teachers, the words on the pages are not for you, but because of you. My husband, our babies, my parents and two rockstar siblings, this incredible team, and you, Mrs. Mac. We were never meant to do any of this alone, and I am so honored and grateful that you chose me to walk home with. xo

Laurie:

The land: I acknowledge with respect and gratitude that my life and work are situated on First Nations, Métis, and Inuit lands. These are the lands of the Blackfoot Nations, including Siksika, Piikani, Kainai, and the Tsuut'ina First Nation. I am grateful for the enduring presence of the Blackfoot Nations on this land.

I acknowledge that we have an ongoing responsibility to protect and honor all life within our shared reality as treaty people and that every child matters. I am called to commit to continuing to learn as I pay respects to the keepers of the land and the land itself.

Our people: Cody, I would not be here if it were not for you. Molly, Casey, and Sadie, I hope your mama made you proud and that you always remember to chase those dreams and not whistle in the house. Thank you doesn't seem like enough, Mom, for everything you do for and with our little family. Julie, you will always be my favorite thing. To my teachers, AJ, Allie, Carly, Michelle, Jacinta, Bryan, Denis, Jana, Marla, Kim, Rieley, Charity, Ainslee, Chelsea, AP, Ms. Fox, Steph, and Rita, thank you for loving me just as I am. To my incredible staff at CSM and the Holy Spirit School Division who have supported me on this journey, thank you for believing in me. Jody, I will forever get hives of gratitude and excitement at the mention of your name. And for every little sweet soul I have ever had the honor of sharing a classroom with, I am who I am because of all that you taught me. I am forever grateful to you.

To our contributors:

What an honor it was to hold your stories. You filled our hearts with inspiration and hope. Thank you for gifting them to us and for sharing your legacies with the world.

We've used your stories to amplify this work.

Natasha Alyward	Tiffany Austin
Nikki Arnott	Susan Barteaux

Acknowledgments

Rhonda Berezowski

Daniele Bourhis

Brittany Chaffin

Terri Grills

Barbara Gruener

Jill Kwasniewski

Nicole Kluthe

Jim Kowalski

Lynn MacDonald

Christy MacNeil

Marlena

Gail Mathias

Lorrie O'Reilly

Kim Patriquin

Darren Pickering

Jen Pilling

Meaghan Reist

Roxanne Riess

Rosalie Roesch

Halee Sikorski

Stephanie Stene

Brenda Stewart

Dr. Scharie Tavcer

Kevin Westwood

Learn from Jody and Laurie

Dr. Jody Carrington

Dr. Jody Carrington is a renowned psychologist sought after for her expertise, energy, and approach to helping people solve their most complex human-centered challenges. Jody focuses much of her work around reconnection—the key to healthy relationships and productive teams.

A speaker, author, and leader of Carrington & Company, she uses all she has been taught in her twenty-year career as a psychologist to empower everyone she connects with. Jody has worked with kids, families, business leaders, first responders, teachers, and farmers and has spoken in church basements and on world-class stages; the message remains the same—our power lies in our ability to acknowledge each other first.

Her approach is authentic, honest, and often hilarious. She speaks passionately about resilience, mental health, leadership, burnout, grief, and trauma—and how reconnection is the answer to so many of the root problems we face. Jody's message is as simple as it is complex: we are wired to do the hard things, but we were never meant to do any of this alone.

With a PhD in clinical psychology, work with major institutions, and a clinical practice, she brings a depth of experience and insight that is unmatched in the industry.

Jody lives in small-town Olds, Alberta, with her husband and three children (she had three kids in two years to test her own resilience) and leads the amazing team at Carrington & Company.

You can find more about Jody, where she's speaking next, her courses, and her other books at drjodycarrington.com, and she's waiting to connect with you on all the hippest social channels.

Laurie McIntosh

Storyteller, light bringer, and dreamer, Laurie McIntosh uses her more than twenty years in education to forge new paths. With the stories she held writing *Teachers These Days* with Dr. Jody Carrington, and her two appearances on *The Ellen DeGeneres Show*, Laurie strives to bring teachers together in community and to define and exemplify what it truly means to be a "teacher these days."

Some of the best lessons are taught in the moments between literacy and numeracy. These golden moments based on kindness, connection, and community are the moments Laurie lives for.

With compassion and thoughtfulness, Laurie has an incredible way of acknowledging the accomplishments of educators and affirms them as they journey on their paths, cheering them on as they use connection and relationship to revolutionize their practice.

You can find all things Laurie at lauriemcintosh.ca or follow her active and awesome commitment to building teachers up across her social platforms.

Kids These Days
A Game Plan For (Re)Connecting With Those We Teach, Lead, & Love
by Dr. Jody Carrington

Learner-Centered Innovation
Spark Curiosity, Ignite Passion, and Unleash Genius
by Katie Martin

Empower
What Happens When Students Own Their Learning
by A.J. Juliani and John Spencer

Unleash Talent
Bringing Out the Best in Yourself and the Learners You Serve
by Kara Knollmeyer

Reclaiming Our Calling
Hold On to the Heart, Mind, and Hope of Education
by Brad Gustafson

Take the L.E.A.P.
Ignite a Culture of Innovation
by Elisabeth Bostwick

Drawn to Teach
An Illustrated Guide to Transforming Your Teaching written
by Josh Stumpenhorst and illustrated by Trevor Guthke

Math Recess
Playful Learning in an Age of Disruption
by Sunil Singh and Dr. Christopher Brownell

Innovate Inside the Box
Empowering Learners Through UDL and Innovator's Mindset
by George Couros and Katie Novak

Personal & Authentic
Designing Learning Experiences that Last a Lifetime
by Thomas C. Murray

Learner-Centered Leadership
*A Blueprint for Transformational Change in
Learning Communities*
by Devin Vodicka

UDL and Blended Learning
Thriving in Flexible Learning Landscapes
by Katie Novak & Catlin Tucker

Made in the USA
Monee, IL
17 August 2021